Afraid
to Tell

Heidi, Tom and Chloe Harding

EBURY
PRESS

1 3 5 7 9 10 8 6 4 2

Ebury Press, an imprint of Ebury Publishing
20 Vauxhall Bridge Road
London SW1V 2SA

Ebury Press is part of the Penguin Random House group
of companies whose addresses can be found at
global.penguinrandomhouse.com

Penguin
Random House
UK

First published by Ebury Press in 2017

www.penguin.co.uk

A CIP catalogue record for this book is available
from the British Library

ISBN 978-1785035180

Typeset in India by Integra Software Services Pvt. Ltd, Pondicherry

Printed and bound in Great Britain by Clays Ltd., St Ives PLC

Penguin Random House is committed to a
sustainable future for our business, our readers
and our planet. This book is made from Forest
Stewardship Council® certified paper.

If reading this book helps just one person who suffered abuse as a child realise that what happened to them was wrong and that they are not alone in the world, then telling our story will have been worthwhile. If it helps someone find their voice and speak out against the sexual abuse of children, we really will believe that what happened to us happened for a reason.

What you see and what you hear depends a great deal on where you are standing.

It also depends on what sort of person you are.

– C.S. Lewis, *The Magician's Nephew*,
from *The Chronicles of Narnia*

This book is a work of non-fiction based on the recollections of the authors. Names of people and places have been changed solely to protect the privacy of others.

This book is all about different perceptions. Therefore, there are a few occasions in what follows where the siblings remember things differently – these have been kept true to their memories.

Why We Wrote this Book

You wouldn't think it was possible for two sisters and a brother to grow up together in the same home, with the same parents, and yet be completely unaware of what's happening to their siblings. It *is* possible, though – we're the proof of that. In fact, because two of the three of us share the 'family trait' of never wanting to talk about our feelings and emotions, we might have lived for the rest of our lives without ever knowing about some of our siblings' most significant experiences as children.

Like most brothers and sisters, we often spent time in each other's company when we were young – eating meals, watching TV or playing together, for example. But, like portrait artists painting the same sitter from different angles, we all had slightly different perspectives on almost every important thing that happened.

We also had very different feelings about the prospect of writing this book, which ranged from fear that the process might trigger unwanted memories, to a sense of duty, to huge relief at the thought that our story was finally going to be told. What surprised us all, however, is that by the time we had finished writing it, those initial feelings had changed, and we began to realise that, in many respects, we weren't as different as we'd always thought we were. Some-times people on a journey can take different routes but still end up eventually at the same destination, together.

We're all approaching or already in our thirties now, and if we hadn't written this book we probably wouldn't ever have understood each other the way we do today, or have realised that the bond between us, which in the past had sometimes seemed strained and uncertain, is actually very strong. That doesn't mean we're always going to agree about everything in the future. We're basi-cally the same people we were before we told our stories, with the same potential, like any siblings, sometimes to be irritating or obtuse. But we have all gained a new kind of confidence from the knowledge that tugging on the bond that binds us – when we annoy each other or disagree about something – *isn't* going to break it.

Things have changed a lot since we were children, and as awareness of the extent and impact of child abuse has in-creased, the processes surrounding disclosure and prosecution have improved significantly. If something bad is happening to you – or to someone you know – we urge you to tell someone, so that you can get the help and support you deserve.

Heidi, Tom and Chloe

Chloe

I was 11 years old when Heidi read my diary. A lot of bad things happened after that, and I was angry with her for a long time because of what she'd done. What I didn't think about until quite recently, however, was *why* she did it.

I'm very much the sort of person who likes to bury the past and leave it buried – forever, if possible. So my immediate reaction when Heidi asked me to tell my side of the story in this book was to say no. Then, when I thought about how important it was to her, I realised that I owed her an explanation of why I responded the way I did to everything that happened as a consequence of what I wrote – and she read – in my diary all those years ago.

It wasn't until we first talked about the possibility of writing our story and I saw something Heidi had written that I became aware for the first time that while I had been blaming her for reading my diary when she knew it was private, she had been blaming herself, too. I had no idea she'd felt responsible for all those years for what *she* saw as her failure to protect me when I was a little girl. Suddenly, I began to wonder what else I would learn – about my siblings and myself – once I had agreed to help Heidi write our story.

Tom

I loved my dad when I was a boy. I think I was a lot like him – in some ways, at least. For example, when I was a younger man, I used to believe, as he always did, that the sole purpose of working was to earn money to spend on alcohol and having a good time. But Dad and I did good things together, too, when I was a kid, like going fishing, which is still one of the greatest pleasures of my life – apart from my family, of course.

Dad always had a circle of friends who thought the world of him. But although he was my mate as well as my dad when I was a teenager, I had already begun to realise that he wasn't the easiest person to get on with. Even so, I couldn't understand why Heidi hated him so much, and for a while I didn't know who to believe when I heard about the terrible accusations that were being made against him.

Now, I feel I owe it to my sisters to help them tell their story, by telling mine.

Heidi

For years, I've asked myself the same question: 'How could I have got it so wrong?' There must have been signs. So how did I miss them? It's been like a physical pain, believing that what happened was all my fault. My fault for not telling anyone there was a reason why I hated my dad. My fault for not being more vigilant. And my fault for thinking everything was all right, when it wasn't. What made the pain even worse, however, was knowing that Chloe was angry with me.

It was only recently – 18 years after I read my little sister's diary – that I first considered the possibility that the reason Chloe seemed to hate me might not be the same as the reason why I hated myself. That's when I finally began to see things from her point of view, and to realise how different something can appear to be when looked at by different people from different perspectives.

I am very grateful to my sister and brother for agreeing to tell their stories in this book. It means a lot to me to be able to tell the truth at last about what happened.

Chapter One

Heidi

The earliest memory I have of my childhood is of something that happened one night when I was seven years old. I'd got it into my head that it happened on the night my little sister was born, but that might be wrong, because Mum had some health problems that were made worse by the pregnancy and she was in hospital for a while before Chloe's birth. So it might have been a few days earlier, while I was still waiting for the little brother or sister I'd been longing for.

There must have been lots of good things that happened before that night. I can't remember them if there were, however hard I try. But I do remember, quite clearly, my dad telling me I could stay up late, after my five-year-old brother Tom had gone to bed, and I know it was dark outside by the time I'd changed into my nightie and pushed my arms into the sleeves of the new, silky pink dressing gown Mum had bought for me.

When I went back downstairs and opened the door to the front room, Dad called me his 'special girl'. Then he told me to lie on the floor and squirted Johnson's baby lotion out of a pink plastic bottle on to my tummy. I remember feeling a bit uncertain and wondering what sort of game we were going to play. But I trusted my dad, without being consciously aware that I did. So even when he pulled up his sweatshirt, lay on top of me and started moving up and down in a circular motion, spreading the baby lotion all over my body as he did so, it didn't cross my mind that he would do anything to hurt me.

He didn't speak while he was playing the new game. And as I lay there, with my head against the door and my back squashed uncomfortably into the rough surface of the carpet, I can remember looking up at the heavy red curtains that were drawn across the windows and wondering if he'd forgotten I was there, as he almost seemed to have done.

I don't know how long I lay on the floor, with my eyes fixed on those curtains, before he eventually stood up and, with his back turned towards me, said, 'Go and wash yourself. Then go to bed.'

Adults do a lot of things that seem inexplicable to a seven-year-old child, most of which, I'd come to the conclusion, it wasn't worth trying to understand. But as I walked slowly up the stairs and climbed into bed, I did wonder why his voice had sounded so different when he told me to go to bed from the way it did when, just a few minutes earlier, he had called me his special girl.

I think it was a few months later when he came into my bedroom to say goodnight and said he was going to teach me to do something called a French kiss. He made it sound as though it was something nice, but it wasn't, because he stank of beer and cigarettes and it made me feel sick when I leaned over the side of the bed and did what he told me to do with my tongue.

Although I was only just eight years old, I'd been begging Mum for some time to let me get my ears pierced, and however much I pleaded or sulked, her response was always the same: 'You're too young. We'll talk about it when you're older. Leave it now, Heidi. I'm not going to change my mind. The answer is no.' But a couple of days after he taught me the French kiss, Dad took me into town to get them done, then bought me a pair of gold stud earrings. And, somehow, I knew that, for reasons I didn't understand, the disgusting kissing and getting the thing I wanted were connected.

I think we were in the room he'd built above the garage the time he told me that if I let him touch me 'down there', he'd buy me the gold ring I'd been asking for, which – like the ear piercing – Mum had said I was too young to have. Although I didn't like the idea of him touching me, it didn't seem such a big deal when I thought about the ring he promised to buy me. After all, I rationalised, doing things you don't want to do is just part of being a child.

I would probably have foregone the ring, however, if I'd known that being touched 'down there' would involve him scooping out of a jar a foul-smelling globule of Vaseline, which he smeared on both of us before rubbing himself on me, then putting his finger inside me. To this day, just the sight of a pot of Vaseline makes me feel physically sick.

* * *

We lived at that time in the same coastal town where Mum's parents had a lovely B&B. Mum and Dad bought their house with a deposit raised by Mum working two jobs. Money was very tight for my parents at that time. So when my dad built a room above the garage, it was supposed to be for renting out. Instead, it became *his* space, where he stored his tools and sound equipment and where he disappeared off to from time to time. I can't visualise the room itself now, I just remember that it was flooded with light, and that I used to lock myself in the toilet next to it, which was very dark by comparison.

I suppose a child's blind faith was one of the reasons why I didn't tell anyone what he was doing to me. He was my dad, my eight-year-old self reasoned, so it must be all right, otherwise he wouldn't do it. Other explanations for not saying anything included the fact that I was scared and confused, that I thought it was proof in some way that I *was* his 'special girl', and, as I got older, because I was afraid of hurting my mum. He had told me not to tell her – 'It's our little secret,' he said – although I didn't know why. Would she be upset if she knew? Or angry? With him? With me? What would my brother say? Or my nan and granddad? Would they hate me, the way I'd begun to hate myself? And how would I even raise the subject in a family where no one ever really talked about anything that mattered?

It was Mum who always put me to bed – except when she was in hospital and my dad or Nan was looking after us. I had a captain's bed when we lived in that house, with wooden sides and a metal ladder. And when he came upstairs to say goodnight, which he always did after Mum had gone back down, Dad's face as he stood beside it was just about level with mine.

Sometimes, he'd come into my room at night and wake me up, then tell me to lie with my bottom resting against the wood and my legs dangling over the side of the bed. He always made me hold a pillow over my face so that I couldn't see what he was doing when he put his head between my legs and licked and kissed me. But I hated the helpless, suffocating feeling of breathing into the pillow even more than I hated what he did to me, and I was always very scared.

I shared that bedroom with Chloe, but she was always asleep when he came in during the night and did those things to me. Often, Mum would be in the kitchen or watching TV downstairs, or even asleep in their bedroom, which was next door to ours, and eventually I began to resent the fact that she didn't know what was happening.

There was one occasion I remember, when Dad called me into the bedroom while Mum and her friend Valerie were in the kitchen, talking and having a coffee together. Mum asked me later, after Valerie had gone, what he'd wanted to talk about. But I didn't tell her the truth. So how could she possibly have known, or even suspected, that her husband was sexually abusing his own daughter? Even today, when there are so many horrific stories in the media about sexual abuse, there are probably very few women who ever look at their husbands and wonder, 'Could he be doing that to our child?'

* * *

It was my dad who wanted to sell the house and take over the running of a pub in a village not far away – when I was almost nine, Tom was six and Chloe was just two years old. The pub was already quite popular before they secured a loan to buy the lease, which must have been several times greater than the mortgage they'd had on the house. The problem was that there were two other pubs in what was quite a sleepy village for most of the year, until the holidaymakers arrived in the summer. Perhaps an even greater problem, however, was the fact that Dad's idea of running a pub was to sit chatting to the customers while drinking all the profits Mum worked so hard and single-handedly to generate.

He was the sort of person who only paid his bills if he had money left over after he'd done all the things he wanted to do, and he didn't have any business sense at all. So while the pub was doing well – thanks mainly to the excellent Sunday roasts and all the other good food Mum cooked and served – he insisted on installing first a snooker room, then an arcade room, spending so much money on those and other 'boys' toys' that it became almost impossible for them to generate enough income to make ends meet.

When they sold the house and took over the pub, we moved into the flat above it, which is where Dad explained to me one day – in graphic detail – all about the birds and the bees, 'Because,' he told me, his words slurred by drink, 'you're old enough to know about it now. But don't tell your mum, or I'll have to go away.'

I can't believe he really thought an eight-year-old child was old enough to be told the facts of life. So perhaps it was just the way he excused it to himself, to make him feel better. Whatever the reason, although I didn't understand most of what he told me, it was the first time I had any clue at all about what he was doing.

I quickly learned to live in dread of him doing anything nice at all, because whenever he did, there was always that fear of what he was going to expect me to do in return. It was an anxiety that ruined my ninth birthday party for me, when my dad dressed up as a clown and handed out treats to all my friends. I hated the way all the other children seemed to love him. And although I don't remember if he did do anything to me after the party, I know I wasn't able to enjoy it because I was worried about what might happen when the table had been cleared and my friends had all gone home.

Things got progressively worse after we moved to the pub and he began to drink even more heavily than he'd done before. He and Mum started arguing a lot, and there were many nights when I lay in bed listening to him shouting and swearing at her, accusing her of having affairs, telling her she was making a fool of herself and calling her a slag, a slut, a bitch and a cow. He used to say horrible things to her. And when it wasn't the sound of his angry voice keeping me awake, it was the dread of him coming into the bedroom and doing things to me that not even a 'reward' of a thousand gold rings could have made right.

He did things to me many times in the bar or arcade room too, when the pub was shut. On one occasion, when we were all upstairs in the flat, Mum asked him to go down to get a mop and a loaf of bread out of the freezer in the storeroom, and he said to me, 'Come down with me, Heidi. I've got some work I need to do down there, so I'll give you the things Mum wants and you can bring them up.'

I felt sick as I followed him down the back steps, past the cellar and into the kitchen. And my instinct was right, because instead of going to the storeroom, he went into the bar, where he told me to lie on the carpet, then pulled down my trousers and pants.

Although I hadn't *ever* wanted him to do the things he did to me, I'd hated them even more since I'd begun to have some vague idea of what he was actually doing. But I was afraid of what the consequences might be if I made a fuss and refused. On that occasion, I was scared, too, in case Mum came down the stairs and saw us.

Dad often reminded me that what he did was 'our secret', and after I stopped believing he did it because I was 'special', he told me – as he'd done when he explained about the birds and the bees – that Mum would be very hurt and he would have to leave if anyone ever found out about it. I was very close to Mum at that time, and I couldn't bear the thought of causing her distress or, despite everything, of the family splitting up for *any* reason, and certainly not because of something I believed I would be responsible for.

So, that day in the pub, I lay on the floor, as he told me to, while he pulled down his own trousers and pants, lay on top of me and rubbed his penis against my genital area. Then, after what was probably just a few minutes, but seemed like an eternity of anxiety, he rolled on to his back and told me to sit on his stomach with one foot on the floor on either side of him.

Many of my memories of that time are inextricably linked to the patterns and colours of curtains and carpets, which is where I would fix my gaze as I tried to make my mind go blank. It didn't work on that day, however, because all I could think about was what would happen if my mum decided to find out for herself why it was taking me so long to come back with the bread.

Eventually, when he told me to go and wash – which he always did when it was over – I got dressed as quickly as I could and ran up the stairs, clutching the mop and a frozen loaf of bread. And although I was relieved when it became apparent that Mum hadn't even noticed how long I'd been gone, I think I was disappointed too.

I have flashes of memory related to specific incidents that occurred during that time. Or perhaps they aren't *single* incidents I'm remembering, but segments of lots of different ones that have all merged together to form a single picture. It's difficult to say which of the horrible things he did to me I dreaded most. Certainly somewhere near the top of the list would be what happened almost every time he had a bath, when he'd tell me, 'Wait five minutes, then come in and wash my hair.' I can still hear in my head the swooshing sound the bathwater made as he stood up to unlock the door, and I still hate the smell of the Vosene shampoo I always used when I washed his hair.

After I'd filled a cup with clean water and rinsed the last few bubbles of shampoo out of his hair, he would tell me to wash his pubic hair and penis with my hand. Then he'd put his own, much larger hand over mine and move it up and down until his penis went hard, which is when he'd say, 'That's enough now. Go and wash your hands.'

One day when he was having a bath, he told me to take off my trousers and pants and stand astride him, facing him, with one foot on either side of the bathtub. As always, I did what I was told, and as I balanced there, anxious and uncertain, he touched my nose with his finger, then traced a path down my body until his hand was between my legs. I don't know what made him suddenly change his mind and tell me to get dressed, but I don't think he ever did the same thing again.

There are lots of things I still hate today that I know are related in some way to what my dad did to me when I was a little girl. Fortunately, apart from Vaseline and the smell of Vosene shampoo, I can't remember the specific reasons why most of the other things make me feel anxious and sick.

It was before we moved to the pub, when we were still living in the house near my grandparents, that Dad gave me a pair of stockings one day and told me to put them on. I didn't, though. I just dropped them on the floor when he handed them to me, then put them in the wash basket in the shower room later, where maybe Mum found them, although I didn't think about that possibility at the time – not consciously, at least. He didn't say anything on that occasion, and a few years had passed before he bought me another pair, when I must have been 11 or 12. I did put them on that time, but I don't have any memory of what happened next. It must have been something particularly unpleasant though, because stockings and suspender belts are other things that give me a horrible sick feeling whenever I see them.

It wasn't all abuse and shouting when we lived in the flat above the pub. We did have some good times there, and I used to love looking after Tom and Chloe every Sunday, while Mum cooked roast dinners for the customers. I'd often make jelly on these occasions, which I'd serve with ice cream to my brother and sister, and Mum too, so that it was like a party – and as close as I ever came to creating the life I so desperately wanted to be living. But even those days sometimes went horribly wrong. Like the time Chloe pulled a kettle of boiling water off the work surface in the kitchen and burnt her foot really badly when I was looking after her, and even the terrible telling-off I got from Mum and Dad couldn't have made me feel any worse than I did already.

I adored Chloe from the first moment I saw her in the hospital the day after she was born, when I was seven. She was a lovely baby, and became a very pretty, caring, nurturing little girl, who loved playing with dolls, and I was never happier than when I was playing with her. But whereas Chloe brought out the mothering instincts in me – even when I was only a little girl myself – Tom was often my 'partner in crime', sometimes as willing accomplice and sometimes as victim when one of my ideas turned out to be rather less bright than I'd thought it was.

One day, for example, just before our parents took over the pub, when I was eight and Tom was six, I told him to ride his BMX bike as fast as he could down the road outside our house. The problem was, the bike didn't have any brakes. 'But it's okay,' I assured him, with all the confidence of a big sister, 'the wall at the end of the road will stop you.' And who knows, I might have been proved right about the bike-stopping qualities of a brick wall if a car hadn't turned out of the car park just as Tom attained maximum speed. By some miracle, he wasn't badly hurt when he smacked into the side of the car, although he might have been.

Tom hit the car on the passenger's side and, while the woman in the passenger seat wound down her window and shouted at him, the man who had been driving got out of the car and walked round it to check the door for damage. Fortunately, there wasn't any, and although he looked angry too, he didn't actually say anything, whereas the woman was very vocal. Then, without either of them asking if Tom was all right, the man got back in the car and they drove off, much to my relief.

Another of the doubtful theories I got Tom to test out was that a large wooden catering tray could be used successfully as a sled on a steep, snow-free, rocky slope. We had moved to the pub by that time and I had a couple more years of experience of cause and effect than I'd had when I instigated the BMX fiasco. I suppose that's why, having initially intended to do it myself, I changed my mind when we reached the top of the hill behind the pub and persuaded Tom to sit on the tray instead of me.

It wasn't until he was actually flying down the hillside, the wooden tray bumping and bouncing over every rock, that I realised it was probably one of the worst ideas I'd ever had. When he reached the bottom of the hill, he almost took off, before landing in a patch of thorns and stinging nettles. The injuries he received that time were even worse than those inflicted by the car when he hit it with his bike, although, fortunately, not bad enough for him to require hospital treatment.

In fact, Tom has always been very lucky – surviving with just a few cuts and bruises when he inadvertently opened the car door and fell out as Dad was driving around a corner, for example. On one occasion, when Mum took us to a village fete and gave us £1 each, I spent my money immediately on ten 10p raffle tickets, while Tom went on every ride and played every game available. Then, two seconds before the raffle closed, he bought a ticket with his last 10p – and won the main prize! Another time, Mum entered us both in a competition that was being run by a children's TV programme, and when they drew the winning entry out of the *three skiploads* of postcards they had in the studio, it was Tom's!

I had a good relationship with my mum when she and – to a much lesser extent – Dad were running the pub. Sometimes I thought my dad had good in him too and that maybe he *could* be like a real dad – on the night when there were very strong winds, for example, and he rushed around the flat securing all the windows, as if he really did care about his family and wanted to protect them. Or the time he rescued a puppy.

I had been walking past some flats behind the pub when I saw the little dog gazing miserably out of the window of one that appeared to be empty. At that time of year – outside the holiday season – several of the flats were occupied by itinerant workers of one sort or another, most of whom came to do seasonal work on local farms. It turned out that one of them had put the dog in the cold, unoccupied flat because they'd got fed up with her making a mess on their floor.

When I told Dad about the puppy, he got the key to the flat from the man who rented out the properties, and came home with her in his pocket. Then, later that evening, he went back and persuaded the people who'd dumped the dog to let us have her. 'They'd given her the name of some drug,' I heard him tell Mum. 'And they've been feeding her on sausages and mashed potato. So it wasn't surprising she was shitting all over the floor. I told them they weren't fit to look after a goldfish, let alone a puppy, and eventually they said I could take her.'

'What are you going to call her?' he asked me when he put the puppy in my arms. And, after thinking about it for a while, I decided to call her Lexi.

Lexi was a tiny terrier mixed with something we didn't ever really manage to identify. For me, she became the one 'person' I could talk to, and I told her everything. It was almost as though she felt grateful for having been rescued, and when I buried my face in her fur and told her about all the unspeakable things my dad had done to me, she would lick my hand as if she was sorry and wanted to make me feel better too.

Although Mum worked incredibly hard when we were at the pub, she still sometimes found time to give me a treat and I always looked forward to the occasions when she'd say, 'Come down this evening, Heidi, and you can sit in the pool room and have a rack of ribs,' which was another popular item on the menu she cooked and served in the bar. Tom and Chloe probably remember that time as being a positive period in their childhood. But despite the fact that we did have some nice times while we were there – or, at least, some nice things happened – it was different for me, because those few good times were far outweighed by the bad.

Night after night, I'd wake up and find him standing beside my bed. And when he'd done what he wanted to do, I'd try to comfort myself with the thought that at least no one else knew that he was doing it, so no one else could be hurt by it. In the daytime, I often ran away, up to the field behind the pub where I fed the horses, or to the top of the steep hillside where no one else ever came and where I could be by myself and think my own thoughts for as long as I chose to stay there.

Although my dad had warned me that no one must know about 'our secret', and I was afraid of what might happen if anyone did find out, I think I sometimes wanted Mum to realise that there must be some reason why I kept running away and to ask me what it was. But she never did. In fact, most of the time no one came to look for me at all, and if I saw him coming, I'd hide so that he couldn't find me.

One afternoon when we were living in the flat above the pub, Mum was working downstairs – as she always was – while

Dad had a nap, and when he woke up he called me into their bedroom. I can still remember standing in the open doorway, my fingers clasped around the door handle, looking at the unmade bed, wishing I didn't have to go in and knowing that I did, because he was my dad and I had to do what he told me to do.

The sun seemed to be trying to force its way in through and around the edges of the drawn curtains as I closed the bedroom door and lay down beside his horrible naked body on the bed. Even though I didn't really understand at first what he meant when he told me to put his penis in my mouth, I said 'No!' and turned away. So he put his hand on the back of my head and pushed it down towards his groin, pressing harder until my neck ached if I tried to pull away. Then he started to push my head up and down. Even when I began to choke, he just forced me down again so that I felt sick and couldn't breathe. And when I did manage to raise my head once, very briefly, I was frightened by the almost-angry expression on his face.

When he ejaculated in my mouth, I thought at first something terrible had happened. But he just handed me a tissue and told me to wipe my face. Then I went into the bathroom and cleaned my teeth, although it didn't seem to matter how many times I washed my mouth out with water, I still felt sick – and very shocked – and couldn't get rid of the disgusting taste and smell of him.

It was an incident that lasted much longer than anything he'd done before, and a couple of days after it, I found a £5 note in my jewellery box. I knew immediately that he had put it there, and that it was part reward, part bribe, to ensure I didn't tell anyone what had happened. And although I still didn't really understand what *had* happened, I think that was when I began to suspect that, whatever it was, it wasn't 'normal' after all.

Chapter Two

Heidi

I was nine years old when I rang Childline for the first time. I think I heard about it on a TV programme, or perhaps I saw a poster somewhere. I can't remember now. But I know it was free to call, and easy to memorise. In fact, it's the same number today – 0800 1111.

I phoned Childline that first time from a phone box in the village. It was a new experience having someone to talk to apart from Lexi and I rang several times after that. But I never said anything about my dad. He had told me so often, 'It's a secret. You mustn't breathe a word to anyone,' that I was far too scared to talk about it, even over the phone to a stranger who didn't know who I was. So I talked about my dog and about how I liked being by myself, while the person on the other end of the line listened, and occasionally said something encouraging. It doesn't sound very significant when I say it now, but, at the time, those phone calls had the strange effect of making me feel almost free, and safe.

My dad was a very angry person and I was very intimidated by him. Although I can only remember one occasion when he hit me, when I was older, around the time I was taking my GCSEs, he started being violent towards my mum when we lived in the flat above the pub, shouting at her and saying horrible things to her – that she was worthless, less than nothing. His most common accusation, however, was that she was cheating on him, which was ridiculous in view of the fact that if she wasn't working, she was either asleep or taking care of us. What made it even more absurd was that he flirted with women all the time and I'm sure he had affairs with some of them over the years, including the waitress who worked at the pub.

Even worse than listening to him shouting at Mum was hearing him dragging her around the flat by her hair. I loved my mum and I was starting to hate him, and lying in my bed late at night, wide awake and anxious, while he hurt her made me feel even more frightened and helpless than I did when he was sexually abusing me.

They hadn't had nearly as many arguments before we moved to the pub. But as the anger and aggression that were already part of his character were further fuelled by alcohol, I would often wake up in the middle of the night to find Mum curled up asleep next to Chloe on the bunk bed underneath mine.

Tom and I had had to move schools when Mum and Dad took over the pub. It seemed daunting when it happened. But the village school we went to was really nice, and as well as making some good friends there, I had a wonderful teacher called Mr Russell, who used to let me walk his dog Bella around the field next to the school at lunchtimes. I was lucky to have those new friends, because the worse my own father became, the more I took refuge in the homes of girls whose fathers talked pleasantly to them and bought them the things they wanted because they loved them, not to keep them quiet. One of the nicest of those fathers was my friend Sally's dad. In fact, both her parents were really good to me and would often take me with them when they went out for the day.

Then, one day, they asked if I'd like to sleep over. When I said I would, they made up a bed for me in their living room on a sun lounger that nearly folded in half in the middle of the night, trapping me in my sleeping bag until morning because I was too frightened to call for help. I realise now, of course, that Sally's dad probably wasn't even aware of the existence of anything as horrible as the sexual abuse of a child by a parent. But I didn't know that at the time, and although I idolised him, I thought that if he came into my room in the night, he might do something to me.

Another good friend I made at that school was a girl called Charlotte, whose parents were quite a bit older than Sally's, and equally kind and gentle. Spending time with both families offered me the chance to escape from my own life for a while. Perhaps even more importantly, it gave me a different perspective on what family life *could* be like, if only I'd had a father like Sally's and Charlotte's, who did *nice* things with me and who really cared whether I was happy or sad.

I didn't ever feel that what my dad did to me and what he made me do to him was my fault – as I know some abused children do. What I did worry about, however, was people finding out about it, partly because I didn't want them to know what I believed was 'the real me', but mostly because of the impact I thought it would have on my family. The way I rationalised it to myself from quite a young age was that as long as I was the only one who was being hurt by what he was doing, everyone else could carry on with their lives and not have to deal with it. In what way it might need to be dealt with, I wasn't clear. I just knew I didn't want my parents to split up – at least, that's the way I felt when I was young. So, eventually, I became very secretive, about everything.

Throughout the time we were at the pub, I was his toy, a means of amusing himself while Mum was working in the pub kitchen or cooking and cleaning upstairs in the flat. And in order to assuage his guilt – or for whatever other twisted reason he did it – he put money in my jewellery box on a regular basis. Every time I opened the lid and saw it there, I had either just done or knew I was going to have to do something I didn't want to do, which made me feel incredibly anxious at the time, and which fills me with disgust when I think about it now.

There were many times when I was a child when I thought it would be better to be dead and not have to do *anything* anymore. I hated my dad for making me feel that way and for eventually making me so afraid of him I didn't dare refuse to do any of the things he told me to do. I didn't really want to be dead, though – I just wanted to have a different, normal life like my friends. In fact, having a normal life was one of the things I used to think about on the many occasions when I sat alone on the hill behind the pub, dreaming about the time when I would be a grown-up, working as a primary school teacher and living in a nice house in the countryside, with a loving husband and two children of my own. And although I thought it was a dream that would probably never become reality, at least it was *something* to hold on to, something to hope for when everything else seemed hopeless.

I was ten when my dad finally drank the pub dry. For three years, Mum had worked as hard as anyone could possibly have done, and while she was working, he was drinking the profits, until eventually, and inevitably, they went bankrupt. I wasn't allowed to tell anyone that we were leaving. In fact, we did a moonlight flit and went to live in a horrible, cold, bare-floored council house that was about half an hour's drive away. As well as being too far to make it easy for me to keep in contact with any of my friends, I was ashamed of our new house, particularly in comparison to the pub, which was in a really nice village. So I didn't really try to keep in touch with them, not even with Sally, who I found out many years later, when we met at a wedding, had been very hurt by the fact that I hadn't confided in her before we left the pub or tried to make contact with her afterwards.

It was a month before the end of my last term at primary school when we moved, which isn't the best time to start at a new school if you're going to have any chance of making new friends. What made it all far worse, however, was that after I'd been there for just a few days, a girl called June, who had a taken an immediate dislike to me, tried to force me off the school bus by chanting,

'Off, off, off!' For the whole journey home, I bit my lip and stared resolutely out of the window, determined not to give her the satisfaction of knowing how close I was to bursting into tears.

In fact, no one made me feel welcome at that school. But why would they? They had friends they'd made seven years ago, or more. Why would they care about someone who was only going to be around for a month before the start of the summer holidays, after which they would all be moving on to secondary schools – new girls themselves this time, but accompanied by at least some of their established friends?

I wrote to my old teacher, Mr Russell, after I left the nice primary school in the village where the pub was, including in the envelope letters for some of my friends. I've never forgotten what he said when he wrote back to me:

Make the best of the future, Heidi. Don't sit around pining for what's in the past. This school, Bella and your friends are all part of the story of your life. Now you must make another chapter to enjoy. I know that you will. It was lovely to have you in my class.

From Mr Russell and Bella

I still get upset, all these years later, when I think about how horrible it was having to leave all the people I was close to at that school, especially in circumstances that must have made them think I'd simply moved on and didn't care about them anymore. I missed their families too, and the chance they'd offered me to escape – if only for a few hours – into a world where people were nice to each other and you didn't have to dread your dad coming into your bedroom at night. I was allowed to get in touch with them again after a while, by which time most people in the village where the pub was had heard the rumours about how my parents had left owing thousands of pounds after my dad had ruined the business. He didn't care, though. He just brushed off the past like someone flicking a speck of dust off their shoulder, then set about reinventing himself, telling our new neighbours in the village we'd moved to whatever story suited his purpose at the time. And within just a few months, they all loved him.

One thing did stay the same after we moved though, and I have a very vivid memory from around that time of Mum being in hospital again and Dad asking me one evening after Tom and Chloe had gone to bed if I wanted to play cards with him. Every time something like that happened, I think I always hoped that *this* time he really did just want to play a game. But although I said yes, I'm sure I knew in my heart of hearts that the game we were going to play wouldn't be the sort of simple, fun card game I played with my friends and their parents when I went round to their houses for tea. And I was right, of course. After telling me to sit on the floor with my back against the door, he smirked as he dealt the cards, then said, 'If you lose in this game, you have to take off a piece of clothing.'

When he was naked and I had nothing on except my socks, he told me to lie down with my head against the door. Then he lay on top of me. I think I was so anxious about the possibility of Tom coming downstairs and banging my head on the door as he tried to open it that I was too focused on listening for the sound of Tom's footsteps to be more than barely aware of what my dad did on that occasion. I just remember him wiping himself afterwards on the tissues he always had to hand.

Dad wasn't a good person, in any respect. Even when we were at the pub, a man with a suitcase used to come round periodically and sell him things like knives and bedding, which he'd stolen from department stores. So although he didn't work after we moved out of the flat and into the council house, he may have been doing something 'on the side'. It didn't prevent him from hanging around the house most of the time though, and I used to walk home from school every day hoping and praying he wouldn't be there.

Perhaps it was the same suitcase-carrying friend who sold him the Commodore Amiga 500 he gave us for our first Christmas in that house. The Amiga was a relatively early type of home computer, which most people used as a gaming machine, and he gave us some games with ours too, including one called Big Nose the Caveman, which is the only one I can still remember. That computer was the best present we could possibly have imagined. I hated everything about my new life – leaving behind all my friends and my school, and moving into what was a really shitty house. But, finally, that Christmas, it felt as though things might be returning to normal – even if it was different from the life we were used to and, in my case, very different from what other girls of my age would have considered 'normal'.

After a couple of years, the computer was one of various items that mysteriously went missing from the house. When I asked Mum and Dad what had happened to it, Mum said she didn't know, and Dad just shrugged. Then, a few days later, when I answered the phone at the house, a man said he was interested in the Amiga 500 he'd seen advertised for sale in the local paper. I think I realised immediately what my dad had done. But even when I showed him the advert circled in yellow that I'd found in a copy of the local free ads paper on the table beside his bed, he still denied all knowledge of it. It was obvious that he was lying – there was no other plausible explanation for the coincidence of the disappearance of the computer he had given us as a Christmas present, the phone call and the encircled advert – and I was really angry. But he could always look you in the eye and tell you, with absolute sincerity, that the chair you were sitting on was red, not blue, as you had believed it to be.

Before we went bankrupt, he had taken everything out of the pub – the washing machine, TVs, everything – and had hidden them in a friend's barn, so that the bailiffs couldn't take them. Apparently, the plan was that after we'd settled into our new home, he'd go back and get them. When the time came, however, he said there'd been a problem and only some of the items were still there. I didn't really think about it until the computer disappeared, which is when it suddenly dawned on me that he'd sold all the things he didn't need himself.

* * *

Things did get better for me when I started secondary school after the summer holiday – *outside* the house, at least. Unfortunately, though, it turned out that June, the girl who had been so mean to me on the school bus during my last few weeks at primary school, had got a place at the same secondary school, and for a while she continued to hate me and tried her best to make my life miserable.

I think it was the rare glimpses I'd had of my dad's good – or, perhaps more accurately, less bad – side that made me believe everyone has *some* good in them. Which is probably why I became determined to turn June from an enemy into a friend. It's a characteristic I still have, of responding to someone who isn't being nice to me by being resolutely and persistently kind to them, until they're almost forced to give in. It took a few months, but eventually I succeeded with June, and it turned out that she was actually a very nice girl. In fact, we're still friends to this day.

Once again, the friends I made at secondary school had wonderful parents, who took me with them on days out and on visits to their relatives in other parts of the country. Meanwhile, at home, my dad continued to do what he'd been doing since I was seven, with one eye on the door when Mum was in the house, but with no holds barred on the several occasions when she was in hospital having treatment for the inflammatory bowel disease she's had for as long as I can remember.

I never slept soundly when I was a child. Some part of my mind was always on the alert, listening and waiting for him to come into my bedroom. And when I did fall asleep, I often had awful dreams. I remember dreaming one night that someone was in the house with a gun, then waking up and trying to slide into the gap between my bed and the wall, unable to work out what was real and what wasn't. I think that dream was probably prompted by the gun my father always kept in the house, and by the knowledge, even at a young age, that a firearm and an angry man who drinks too much are a potentially dangerous combination.

I don't remember a time when I didn't hate and fear my dad in almost equal measure. But it wasn't until I was in the second year of secondary school and we started having sex education lessons that I began to realise that what he was doing was completely wrong and that no man should ever do those things to any child, let alone a father to his own daughter.

After we moved from the pub, Mum got a job in a shop in town, while Dad occasionally sang in pubs and clubs or provided sound systems for classic car shows, country fairs and similar events, all the time claiming state benefits. Mum's parents, my nan and granddad, lived about half an hour's drive away, so I would sometimes go and stay with them for a few days during school holidays and for weekends. I loved staying at their house – it was always tidy and clean, and I felt safe there. Nan seemed to know how to do everything just right, and whenever I stayed with her, or she came to our house to look after us when Mum was in hospital and Dad was 'busy', she'd give me my dinner on a tray, laid out nicely with a napkin and just the right amount of food. Then she'd bring me a cup of warm milk and let me stay up to watch *Coronation Street* with her, before giving me a cuddle and kissing me goodnight when I went to bed.

Nan has always been one of my best friends. She and Granddad had a way of making you feel as though you mattered, which was in complete contrast to the way Dad always made me feel. The only person that seemed to matter to him was him, and I can remember sitting at the dining table on several occasions after the bankruptcy, watching him devour the steak he'd bought for himself while we ate whatever Mum had been able to scrape together for us. It was becoming increasingly difficult to believe that he had any good in him at all, and as each year passed, I hated him more and more.

I was nine when I started keeping a diary, which was a habit I continued, on and off, for the next few years. 'Mum's granddad's sister died,' I wrote one day, 'and HE told me to go upstairs. I hate him. I wish he was dead because he's ruined my life.'

And later:

Dad was going on about the law and courts. It was so boring. He was going on about how people mess up their lives, not knowing what they're doing. He can't talk. Pig. I hate him. He's ruined my life. I asked him if I could have a packet of crisps –

Monster Munch. He said, 'Give me a cuddle and I'll give you some crisps.' So, stupid me, I did. And guess what? He did it again. He started feeling me around my bust. I've never written about this in my diary because I was scared. But I have to get it out. I used to think I'm in a coma and it was all a dream. Now who do I turn to? I'm stuck. When I was little he did all sorts of things to me. I just don't know what to say. It hurt so much. He would bribe me to do horrible things, then give me a fiver … I hope he feels guilty. I can't tell anyone. I'm scared he will hurt me or Mum, or Chloe or Tom. I don't wish I was dead. But I do wish I was one of my friends with a normal life. I cried myself to sleep last night. This will affect my whole life. I wanted to have a great life, a normal life … HELP.

I was 13 when that incident with the crisps occurred, and I can remember feeling almost more angry about it than I had been about anything he'd done to me before. It was one of only a few times I wrote about him in my diary, and after I'd become aware that what he was doing was wrong and not something other fathers did to their daughters, I began to confront him. I remember saying to him on one occasion, 'If you *dare* do anything to me …' I didn't finish the sentence, but I think he knew that I would eventually tell someone and that it wasn't safe for him to abuse me anymore. So although I don't remember there being a specific moment when it stopped, I think it wasn't long after that, and I think *he* was the one who stopped it.

Everyone assumed that my apparent hatred for my dad was just part of being an angst-ridden teenager, albeit one who was even more troubled and prone to angry moods than most teenagers tend to be. But the hatred was real and the fundamental reasons for it weren't puberty related at all: I hated him, pure and simple. And I hated the fact that everyone seemed to think he was 'such a good guy', when in reality he was a self-serving, self-engrossed, child-abusing bully.

I used to say things to him in front of other people like, 'You're going to die an ugly, lonely old man. If you had a walking stick, I would kick it out from underneath you.' Which only made them feel sorry for him and wary of me. What really hurt, however, was that my mum never stuck up for me when I argued with him. I can remember asking her once *why* she didn't. But I suppose it was for the same reason that she never fought back against him. Perhaps she was even more intimidated and scared of him than I was.

What also used to upset me was the fact that Mum didn't ever seem to wonder *why* I said such horrible things to him and hated him with such vehemence. I can understand other people putting it down to teenage angst. 'But surely,' I thought, 'she should realise – or at least suspect – that something else might be wrong?'

It didn't really matter though, because even if she *had* tried to talk to me about it, I wouldn't have told her the truth. In my teenage mind, I was a 'superhero' and it was my responsibility to suffer in order to save my family. I just wished they didn't hate me the way they increasingly seemed to do.

Chapter Three

Heidi

My father was a very bossy man, and as well ironing his shirts, I used to have to make him endless cups of tea, which I would spit in before wiping his piece of cake on the kitchen floor, before taking them into the lounge and dumping them on the little table next to the sofa, where he would be sitting watching TV.

From the age of seven, I'd felt trapped and confused. When I was 14 and really understood what he'd been doing, I was just angry – with everyone. The one comfort I had during that period was spending time in the beautiful cathedral in town. I used to go there after school and wander around under the sweeping curves of its stone pillars, reading all the notices about service times, music recitals and all the other events that were advertised or took place there. Sometimes, I'd light a candle and sit on a pew, where, surrounded by space and quietness, I'd release the breath it felt as though I'd been holding for years. It was sitting in that cathedral – where no one intruded on my solitude or spoke to me unless I spoke to them – that gave me a love for old churches that I still have today. I felt safe there, in a way I couldn't ever remember having felt before.

As soon as I was old enough, I got a paper round, which I loved. The thing I liked most about it, in fact, was walking around the village in the quiet of the early mornings, before most other people were up, which is another pleasure that has stayed with me. I still walk for miles almost every Sunday morning, alone with my thoughts, working things out in my head and enjoying the sense of freedom it gives me.

After the paper round, I got a job in a cafe in town, where I washed up from 9 a.m. until 5 p.m. every Saturday and Sunday, and on several other days of the week during school holidays. I had to wear a black skirt and white blouse for that job, which I hated to begin with, because I was skinny and lacking in confidence, and also because I'd always worn trousers since the Christmas Day I came downstairs in my new tartan skirt and my dad put his hand up inside it. But if I didn't wear the uniform, I wouldn't get the job, so Mum took me to a factory shop and bought me a skirt and blouse, and I paid her back from what I earned.

Working at the cafe involved getting a bus into town and back every Saturday and Sunday. So after I'd worked there for about a year, I got a job in the local village pub instead – just a short walk away from home – washing up on Saturdays and doing the cleaning every Sunday. I was still doing that job a couple of years later when I got another one, stacking shelves in a supermarket in town every weekday morning before school. Then I dropped the job in the pub to work on the tills in the same store.

I liked working – being by myself all the time, self-sufficient, and out of the house so that I didn't hear Mum and Dad's increasingly bitter rows or the nasty, aggressive things he said to her. The only problem was that being out of the house so much made it very difficult for me to do the other 'job' I'd set myself some time ago, which was to watch Chloe like a hawk to make sure my father couldn't do to her what he'd done to me. I remember that I was standing by the window in the living room one day when we heard Chloe come into the house and go upstairs and I told him, 'If you ever dare touch her, I'll kill you.' He probably didn't realise that I meant it, but he must have known it would be the one thing that would make me tell someone what he'd done to *me*.

Although things had deteriorated between Mum and Dad, there was one night when I was 16 and we all went to a dance at the local village hall. Mum was wearing a red dress and Dad asked the DJ to play the song 'Lady in Red'. Then he and Mum danced together, while everyone watched them and thought how romantic it was. I'm sure all those onlookers would have been shocked if they'd known that, within a couple of hours, when Mum and Dad got home, he'd be shouting at her and dragging her round the room by her hair.

Seeing them touching each other and dancing a lie like that made me feel physically sick, and I still can't bear to listen to that song today. Although I could understand why *he* wanted to pretend everything was normal, the question that kept going through my mind was why was she dancing with the enemy? I remember thinking, 'I can't sit here and watch this.' But it was almost like being a voyeur at a car crash or some other terrible disaster – you want to look away, but you feel as though you're frozen to the spot.

I think I felt that, by pretending everything was all right between them, she was almost excusing his horrible behaviour. Saying, in effect, that it didn't matter how many times he got drunk and shouted at her, she'd just keep on forgiving him. So when she told me one day not long after we'd been to that dance that they were going to get divorced, I had to stop myself shouting 'Yes!' out loud.

That night, Chloe and I moved into the front bedroom with Mum, and he moved into our room. Although I was beyond glad that they were finally going to split up, I felt sorry for Mum. She and Dad had been married for about 18 years and I knew it wasn't going to be easy for her, having to deal with whatever would be involved in the divorce. But *she* was the one who had a job, while he didn't contribute anything very much to the household, as far as I could see. So although it would be an ending for her in some ways, it would be a new beginning too: for her, and for me. It was a prospect that lifted my spirits every time I thought about it, and I was furious with her when she told me, two weeks later, that they'd decided to 'give it another try'.

And they did try for a few days. Then everything returned to normal. He accused and abused her, she defended herself as best she could, and I lay awake every night, listening and hating him with ever-increasing passion.

A few months later I did my GCSEs. I'd been predicted Bs and Cs in all of them, but by the time I sat my exams, I was so stressed I was finding it very difficult to concentrate.

Although the abuse had stopped by that time, I suppose the anxiety that had been building up for years was bound to take its toll eventually, in some form or another. But I hadn't realised I'd done as badly as I had, and when I went into school to get my results and found that I'd got one B and all the rest were Ds, I was devastated.

As well as being disappointed with myself for not doing as well as I could and should have done, I knew my results weren't good enough for me to achieve my ambition of going to college and becoming a nurse – which had taken the place of being a teacher in the normal life I imagined having one day. I can remember sitting on the bus on the way home, staring out of the window without seeing anything, thinking, 'Things couldn't be any worse.' But I was wrong, because what hurt even more than feeling as though I'd let myself down and that I was going to have to rethink my entire future was the fact that when I did get home, no one asked me how I'd done.

I knew that the anger I had towards my dad sometimes made me difficult to live with, and I'd often felt like an outsider in my own home, but I hadn't ever felt quite as lonely and hopeless as I did that day. It wasn't the first time I'd thought I wouldn't care if I died, but it *was* the first time I really meant it.

Apart from wounding my pride and shaking what little confidence I had left, not getting the GCSE grades I needed to become a nurse worked out all right in the end. After I'd got my exam results, I went to the local college to find out what I *was* qualified to do, then enrolled on an office skills course that started in the September. For the rest of the summer, I continued to work in the pub and to spend most of my free time with my new boyfriend, Sam, who lived in the village next to ours and who I'd had a crush on for some time before we started going out.

Even though Sam was a kind and gentle person and we did have sex, I didn't ever tell him about what my dad used to do. I still didn't really understand it myself. Sometimes, after one of my solitary vigils in the cathedral, I'd go to the library in a nearby street to look for books that might shed some light on it. The problem was that although I did find several books about sexual abuse, I couldn't risk checking any of them out and taking them home: what if someone saw them, or, worse still, saw me reading one of them?

Then, one day, I noticed a leaflet on a table in the library about a local charity offering support to people who had been raped or sexually abused and I copied down the helpline number – surreptitiously, while pretending to study the noticeboard that was tacked to the wall above the table. I don't know what would have happened to me if I hadn't found and phoned that number when I did. I'd got to the point of feeling that I couldn't cope anymore. I thought everyone in my family hated me, so I continued to push them away, then felt lonely and isolated. I was envious of – as well as thankful for – my friends, whose families so obviously loved and cared about them. 'It's your fault,' I used to tell myself. 'Your friends are *nice* people. That's why their families love them.'

I seemed to be facing a completely blank wall, and I was tired of feeling angry. In fact, I thought almost constantly about ways I could put an end to it all, and would often do things like holding my breath underwater in the bath, wishing I was brave enough not to splutter and fight my way to the surface every time I almost blacked out, or stand at the side of the road, imagining stepping out in front of buses, cars or trains. 'Just do it,' the voice in my head would say. But, again, I wasn't brave enough.

'It isn't fair,' I used to think. 'All I'm trying to do is protect everyone else by keeping the secret that's slowly poisoning me from the inside, whereas what's actually happening is that I'm making everyone's life miserable, including my own.'

Sometimes, it felt as though, if I didn't do *something*, I was going to explode into a million pieces. Then the *other* voice in my head would say, 'If I can just keep going, I can beat this.' What I'd begun to realise, however, is that I couldn't beat it on my own. So I phoned the number on the leaflet I'd seen in the library and, suddenly, I had someone to help me.

The woman who answered the phone told me, 'The charity has only just been set up, and we're still very small, but we *do* have an office. I can meet you outside it at 4.30 tomorrow afternoon, if that time's suitable for you?'

'Yes, that's fine,' I told her.

'Okay, great,' she said. 'Well, my name's Lesley. I'm quite tall with dark wavy hair, and I'll be wearing a blue dress.'

I recognised her immediately when I saw her standing outside the office building, waiting for me, at 4.30 the following afternoon. She looked nice. But as I watched her from the doorway of the department store across the road, I began to think, 'I don't need any help with this. It might be harder than it's been before, but I can still do it on my own.' So I didn't cross the road, and having waited for me for a good 20 minutes, Lesley finally gave up and went inside.

As soon as I saw the door close behind her, I regretted not having taken the opportunity to talk to her about the thoughts that swirled constantly around in my head until I was convinced that leaving the earth was my only viable option. As I turned and walked away, I felt incredibly lonely, as if the things that had been done to me had separated and disconnected me from everyone else, so that I was invisible to all the other people on the busy street who were hurrying past me on the way to catch their buses or do some last-minute shopping before heading home.

A week later, having finally accepted the fact that even superheroes sometimes need help, I rang the number again and left a message saying I was sorry I'd missed my appointment and that I'd ring back when the office was manned, because I'd like to make another.

I did meet Lesley at the second attempt, and I saw her for an hour every Wednesday afternoon for a long time after that. In fact, she has been my counsellor and my friend ever since. I didn't talk to her about my dad to begin with, though. I just sat there for the first few sessions, eating sweets and skirting around the issue, until I felt I could trust her enough to tell her the terrible secret I hadn't ever told anyone before.

I was always very tired and zoned out after those sessions with Lesley. It was as if my brain was so overloaded it had simply stopped working, and I never remembered anything about the bus journey home. Then, the next day – when I suppose my subconscious had had a chance to process what we'd talked about – I would feel much better.

I didn't just talk to Lesley about the abuse I'd suffered at the hands of my dad. I told her about my other 'issues' too, such as how I missed having the close relationship I used to have with Mum, and how lonely and confused I felt because I wasn't getting the love and affection I longed for.

Mostly, I talked and she listened. 'You've got the ability to self-counsel,' she told me, quite early on. After a while I realised that she was right, and that when I reflected on something I'd told her, I was able eventually to work out for myself why it had happened and what I could learn from it that would help me to understand it and move on. Learning to counsel myself made me feel stronger, because at last I was *doing* something rather than simply waiting passively for all the worries and anxieties to overwhelm me.

Ever since I'd watched the film *Matilda* when I was a little girl, I'd believed I had special powers like she did, and that I'd been chosen for what was happening to me because I could make something good come out of it. As the years passed and there was still nothing good to be found in any of it, I continued to cling to the same belief and to tell myself, 'This is happening to me because, in some way, I can make a difference. I can *do* something with this.'

So when Lesley told me she thought I was able to self-counsel, it almost felt as though that was my equivalent to Matilda's telekinetic powers and that, like the little girl in the story, I could use and improve on that ability to make it all come right in the end.

Whenever I felt overwhelmed and needed a break – the day my dad hit me, for example – I used to go and stay for a few days with my nan and granddad. It was while I was staying with them on one occasion and had just got off the bus in town one morning, on my way to my shelf-stacking job at the supermarket, that I saw a woman walking towards me crying. I didn't recognise her at first, and I was shocked when I realised it was my mum. She was on her way to work too, looking very tired and dishevelled, as though she hadn't slept.

'Mum?' I wanted to hug her, but she isn't a hugger, and even though I felt like crying myself at the sight of her tear-stained exhaustion, I was afraid of being rebuffed. So I just put my hand on her arm as I asked her, 'Mum, what's happened? What's wrong?' I knew the answer would have something to do with him, but I wasn't expecting her to say, 'Your dad and I are getting divorced. And this time it's final.'

'I know where there's a solicitor,' I said quickly, as if wanting to capture the moment and make her decision ir-revocable. 'Let me make an appointment for one day after work. I can go with you. It'll be all right, I'm sure it will.'

Everything happened quite quickly after that. Mum had moved into the middle bedroom with Dad when she changed her mind the first time about getting divorced, and that night she moved back in with Chloe and me. Then I made an appointment with a solicitor called Mrs Hendry, who I knew about because she had an office in the same building as Lesley's, and within just a few days Dad had been served with divorce papers – outside the village pub, appropriately enough, as it was where he spent a lot of his time, drinking Stella and fuelling his paranoid aggression.

I was dreading him coming home that night, but, in fact, he wasn't as angry as I thought he'd be. It was almost as if he'd been caught on the back foot while making plans of his own, so he didn't see being served with divorce papers as a particularly big deal.

Mum and I had spent that day looking at places for us to move to – nice houses, all of them, including one that had windows in the kitchen roof that filled the room with light and seemed to epitomise what our new life was going to be like. The thought of living in a house where nothing bad had ever happened to any of us, where Mum hadn't been sworn at or threatened, and where I hadn't been abused and intimidated by my own father, filled me with optimism.

Chapter Four

Heidi

We didn't end up moving out of the house that held so many horrific memories for me. The solicitor advised Mum to stay put, for the time being at least, so that when the divorce went through she wouldn't be seen as having voluntarily abandoned any right she had to live there. So Dad stayed in the room I used to share with Chloe, smoking cigarettes and drinking beer. A couple of months after the divorce was finalised, Mum went back to court because he refused to leave the house and, at last, after what seemed like an eternity but was actually about nine months since she had set things in motion, he was forced to move out.

By the time Mum and Dad split up, Tom and I were going through a phase of arguing quite a lot. Most of it was just the usual sibling stuff, although possibly exacerbated by the fact that he loved his dad and couldn't understand why I seemed to hate him so much. Despite our quarrels, however, I was very upset when my brother said, 'I'm going with him.'

I didn't want Tom to go, although not because I feared for him in any way. I never feared for Tom. He seemed to have an ability I didn't have to block things out completely.

And although I knew when I was lying awake at night listening to our parents arguing with each other that he was awake too, he always resisted any attempt I made to talk about it, as if he had no interest in what they were doing.

Despite being upset, I wasn't really surprised that Tom chose to go with his dad when he moved out. He went everywhere with him when he was a boy, doing gardening jobs with him at weekends, going fishing with him or helping him set up his sound systems at various events. In fact, Tom was very like his dad in some ways. Not that he was ever cruel or unkind; he just had the same attitude towards work and money, which was to spend everything you earn on having a good time. I *would* have been worried if I'd known what sort of place his dad was taking him to, but my main concern at the time was Chloe.

Without revealing the secret I'd been keeping for more than ten years, I couldn't tell Mum why I was so vehemently opposed to the idea of Chloe visiting Dad after he and Tom moved out. I told her, instead, 'You shouldn't let Chloe go there because he's violent, and she's only ten years old.' But he hadn't ever hit Chloe – and had only hit me once – and as long as Tom was there as well, I knew she'd actually be all right in that respect. What I was really afraid of was her staying with him overnight, or of her being there at some other time when Tom wasn't.

I think I was quite vocal and persistent in expressing my concerns to Mum, and she must have realised that there was some sense in what I was saying, because although he took Chloe out for a meal occasionally, I don't think she ever slept at the flat. Even so, having thought that I'd been keeping her safe for the last few years, I hated the prospect of not being able to control what happened when she was out of the house.

I don't know how much is innate and how much is the result of spending seven years of my childhood being abused and manipulated by my father so that I felt as though I had no say in anything at all, but I do know that I have a tendency to be a bit controlling. All right, maybe more than 'a bit'. I can't help it, though. Having spent all those years not understanding what he was doing and not being able to stop him doing it when I wanted to so desperately, it's as if I *have* to know everything about what's going on, even if it involves snooping in a way other people would find unacceptable.

Snooping did have its advantages, however. For example, it was going through my mum's papers one day, when I was about 14, that led to the discovery that one of her deceased relatives had left £4,000 to Mum's eldest child – which was me – and that the money had been used to buy Premium Bonds, which my dad controlled.

I waited a few days before I told him, 'I know about the money. It's mine and I want it.'

'You might get it, you might not,' he said. But, much to my enormous surprise, he did sign it over to me after they were divorced – I can only assume because he was afraid I'd tell someone if he didn't – and I bought my first car with the money I got from those Premium Bonds.

Mum must have known I went through her papers, but she never said anything about it. She didn't ever mention their rows either, although she must have been aware that I used to sit at the top of the stairs, listening to him shouting at her.

It was the year I did my GCSEs and I had just started college after the summer holidays when Dad and Tom moved out. I was busy doing my own thing, and didn't give much thought to where they were living. I was going out with Sam at the time, and suddenly life seemed to open up for me. I did work experience as a receptionist at a media company while I was at college, which I really enjoyed. But I hadn't been there very long when my paternal grandma died.

It took the best part of a day to drive to Dad's parents' house, so we hadn't seen them very often when I was young, especially after Chloe was born, when long car journeys with two young children and a baby would have been more difficult. I visited them on my own a few times when I was a teenager though, and they were always really nice to me. Grandma was a wonderful person, and Granddad was very funny, and although my cousin Geraldine told me that Granddad used to beat my dad with a belt when he was a boy and lock him in the coal shed when he did something wrong, I never sensed that in him, and I wasn't ever afraid of him.

Travelling by coach to the town where they lived took more than 12 hours, and every time I set out on the journey home again, I would be carrying a massive cool bag, which Grandma had filled with food for me – so much food, in fact, that on one occasion the strap of the bag broke under the weight.

Grandma loved her boys – my dad and his two brothers, Harry and George – and I knew it would have broken her to know the truth. So of course I never told her what Dad was doing to me. I didn't say anything to Geraldine either, even when she told *me* something that might have prompted me to confide in her. Geraldine was my Uncle Harry's child, and although I didn't see her very often, because they also lived some distance away from us, we got on well when we did meet, and it was lovely when she came to stay with our grandparents while I was there, particularly because we shared a bed and were able to talk late into the night.

Then, one night, she asked me, 'Can I tell you something, Heidi?'

'Yes, of course,' I answered, wondering what she might be about to say, but never imagining for a moment it would be that her dad had come into her bedroom one night when she was asleep and tried to touch the inside of her thigh. She didn't say when it had happened or how old she'd been. Just that, 'I told him to eff off.' And as I was trying to think of something appropriate to say in response, I can remember wishing I'd been able to say that to *my* dad at any time during the seven years he had abused me.

Grandma was the first member of my family to die, and the thought of her not being around anymore was unimaginable and horrible. It felt as though I'd lost one of the very few people in my family who didn't think I was hateful.

The day before the funeral, Dad turned up at our house in a brand new car, which he'd hired to take us all there. It was completely out of character for him to do something like that, something that, on the face of it, wasn't purely for his own benefit. Apart from once staying in a crappy caravan at a campsite just a few miles from where we lived, he had always spent his money on himself and had never splashed out in any way for us. Looking back on it now, however, I wonder if maybe it wasn't an altruistic gesture after all and that he did hire the car for his own purposes – to show Mum, Chloe and me what we were missing, or maybe so that everyone at the funeral would see it and think he was doing well. What might tie in with the first possibility is the fact that I don't remember him saying anything unpleasant to Mum throughout the whole journey.

He'd brought a CD with him and, after we'd all clambered into the car, he played the same track over and over again, looking at us in the rear-view mirror as he sang along with Sweetbox to 'Everything's Gonna Be Alright'. Then, when we stopped at a service station, he bought us all breakfast, which was something else he'd never done before. Suddenly, it felt as though we were on a real family outing, which was an alien but wonderful experience, and as we were eating our breakfast, I can remember thinking, 'Maybe he's changed. It's horrible to be going to Grandma's funeral, but maybe her death has made him see the error of his ways and he realises at last that he should be looking after his children.' Which just goes to prove that, sometimes, hope really does triumph over experience.

My dad and his brother George had fallen out after George put his life savings into some sort of business they'd started together and then accused Dad of taking money out and spending it on the same thing he spent all his money on – alcohol, cigarettes and having a good time. Dad always swore it was rubbish, but, knowing him, I wouldn't be at all surprised if it was true. Certainly George believed it had happened, and after they'd argued, they didn't have any contact with each other at all. Now, though, they would both be staying in their parents' house the night before the funeral.

Dad and Uncle George started drinking almost as soon as we arrived, and it wasn't long before they were arguing and shouting at each other and, once again, I was lying in bed listening to the sound of angry voices. This time, though, I was thinking anxiously, 'This has all gone horribly wrong. What they're doing isn't right. Not today. Not in Grandma's house.'

It must have been around midnight when I heard the front door slam. But although the shouting had stopped, I stayed awake for a long time that night, frightened by what had happened and anxious in case whoever had left the house came back and it all started again.

When I went downstairs the next morning, Mum told me it was my dad who'd left in the night, after George had threatened him with a knife. I liked my Uncle George – although Mum always said he and Dad were as bad as each other – and I've always thought that, to be upset enough to have a fight like that in his parents' house the night before his mother's funeral, he must really have believed that his brother had stolen his money, probably with some justification.

It turned out that what had fuelled their argument – apart from resentment and too much alcohol – was that my dad hadn't gone to the funeral parlour with the rest of his family that afternoon to see his mother's body. Now it looked as though he might not go to the funeral either. But he did turn up at the crematorium, and no one mentioned what had happened.

It probably sounds like an odd thing to say, but Grandma's wake was lovely, because everyone was talking about her and reminiscing about nice or funny things she'd done. Then, when it was over, Dad drove us home again. I don't remember anything about that journey, except for sitting in the car glaring at the back of his head, thinking, 'He hasn't changed at all. He is who he is, and that's the way he'll always be.' It was obvious that his frame of mind was different too, and there was no singing along to Sweetbox and no breakfast at a service station on the long drive home.

Except for the jewellery he used to buy for me as bribes, or rewards, or whatever they were supposed to be – and, on one occasion, a Madonna cassette, which he left in my room with a £5 note tucked inside it – Dad never bought anything for any of us. Mum did all of that. So I was surprised, as well as disgusted, when he turned up at the house with Tom the Christmas after Grandma had died, laden with presents. It was as if he was saying, 'Here I am, living the bachelor life with my son, with plenty of money to splash out on Christmas presents to show you what you're missing.'

I'd hated Christmas since the year he'd put his hand up my tartan skirt, and I'd gone upstairs when I heard him arriving. But Mum made me come down and unwrap the massive Babe the Pig he'd bought for me. And although I hated that pig with a vengeance, it did serve a useful purpose, because I used to kick it around my bedroom as an outlet for all the hatred and anger that was seething inside me.

By the time he bought me that pig I had changed my surname to Mum's maiden name. She didn't question me at all when I told her it was what I wanted to do. She knew I hated the way he treated her and I suppose she thought I was doing it because of the divorce, whereas the real reason was because I didn't want to have any connection with him at all, which seemed possible once Grandma had died and wouldn't be hurt by it. It was easier to keep it a secret from Granddad than it would have been from her, and I didn't talk to Chloe about it either, until a few years later. Then a couple of years after I'd changed my name, Mum changed hers too.

It only cost a few pounds, which seemed a small price to pay for the incredibly liberating feeling of signing his surname for the last time, then writing my new signature – Heidi Harding. Now I had a surname I could be proud of, which was the same name as Mum's dad, who I was always very close to.

After Tom and Dad had moved out, I'd moved into the back bedroom, which Mum helped me to redecorate. But although it was fun painting it with her, splashing my hair with white paint from the roller as I did the ceiling, then laughing as we tied carrier bags over our heads, I still hated that room. In fact, I hated every room in that house because of the memories they held of what he'd done to me, memories I knew couldn't ever be erased, no matter how many times we changed the colour of the walls and hung new curtains at the windows.

I kept asking Mum if we could move and make a fresh start somewhere else, but she always said no, for reasons I never understood. I was angry with her for thinking that redecorating could make it better, although, of course, she didn't know about the worst of the memories at that time. As far as she was concerned, he'd gone, the arguments had stopped, the walls had been repainted, the curtains had been replaced, and we *had* moved on – mentally, if not physically. She must have wondered why I was making such a fuss. In fact, she still lives in that house now, and I still find it difficult every time I visit her there. Maybe houses don't hold memories for her, the way they do for me.

My unwanted present from my dad the following Christmas was a red velvet box containing a gold bracelet and necklace in the shape of a snake. I didn't want anything from him at all, and what made it even worse was that it reminded me of the jewellery he'd bought for me when I was a little girl. And I knew he'd only given me the necklace and bracelet to make a point: 'This is what you're missing by living here with your mother, who can't afford to buy you expensive presents like

I can.' But the only reason *he* could afford it was because he was working at the same time as claiming state benefits. So the point he was trying to make was rather lost in dishonesty.

As soon as the shops opened again after Christmas, I took the red velvet box and its contents to a pawn shop in town, where I exchanged it for £80, which felt as though it was burning a hole in my purse for the brief period of time it was in there before I gave it to charity.

I had been keeping a diary every year for the last 18 or more years, but I didn't write much in it until the following December, when I was in my second and final year at college and broke up with Sam. We had been together for three years and breaking up with him was awful. It wasn't my decision – I still adored him. But he had found someone else, so that was that. There was nothing I could do except try to move on and hope that somewhere, some day, there would be another Sam, however unlikely that seemed at the time.

If I hadn't met Lesley when I did, I don't know how I'd have dealt with the terrible thing that happened in January, a month after Sam dumped me. In fact, I don't know whether I'd have been able to deal with it at all.

Chapter Five

Heidi

Not long after Chloe had left the house one day to walk down to the village shop with a friend, the phone rang, and when I answered it, a woman from the local garden centre asked, 'Have you got a little white and brown terrier?' I said that we had and, after hesitating for a moment, she told me, 'I'm afraid it's been hit by a car on the road just outside the garden centre. I thought it might be yours. Someone's bringing it down to your house.'

'Okay. Thank you,' I said, then went to find a blanket to wrap Lexi in so that I could take her to the vet.

A few minutes later, the front doorbell rang and when I opened it, expecting to see someone carrying little Lexi in their arms, I was taken aback to find a man standing there holding a carrier bag.

'I'm sorry,' the man said. 'She just ran out into the road in front of me – I didn't have a chance to stop.'

'Where is she?' I asked, looking past him to his car and wondering why he seemed to be offering me the carrier bag, as if he wanted me to take it.

'She's here,' he answered. 'She's ... Oh ... Oh, I'm so sorry. Didn't they tell you when they rang? I'm afraid she's dead.'

I don't have any memory of what happened after that. For the last seven years, Lexi had been my companion, my confidante – the only one I'd ever had until I found Lesley – and my best friend. I couldn't believe she was dead. She must have got out of the house somehow and tried to follow Chloe and her friend, who probably would have been too far ahead to have seen her even if they had turned around for some reason.

Completely devastated, I sobbed as I helped Mum dig a hole in the garden and then bury my little dog. I was 18, in my final year of college, doing work I enjoyed and that made me feel as though I had taken the first step on a road that might actually lead to the sort of life I wanted to have. Then, within the space of just a few months, Grandma and Lexi had died, Sam had broken up with me, and everything I thought I'd been building seemed to be coming crashing down. For years, I'd felt as if I'd been swimming constantly against a tide and that every time I thought it was about to subside, it just got stronger and stronger until I was certain I was going to drown. This time, if it hadn't been for Lesley, I don't think I would have survived.

One day, after I'd learned to trust Lesley completely, she took me to meet a very nice, 'normal' woman called Debbie who was about six years older than me. She lived in a lovely house with her husband and beautiful baby, but had had childhood experiences very similar to mine. As we sat there in her living room that first time, drinking coffee and talking, I began to realise that although I couldn't erase the abuse I'd suffered and that it would always be an indelible part of me, it didn't have to define me. That was why Lesley had taken me there, of course: she wanted me to know I hadn't been the only child in the world to have been abused by her father, and she thought that if I saw the happy life Debbie had created for herself despite what had happened to her, I would realise that I could do that too. She was right, because meeting Debbie – which I did again a couple of times after that – did have an impact on the way I saw myself and the life that might lie ahead for me.

Although Chloe had her own bedroom after Tom and Dad left, she slept most nights in Mum's bed. And despite the fact that she was 11 and I was 18, so wouldn't have wanted to sleep in my mum's room, it somehow seemed to emphasise the fact that they were close, while I didn't really speak to anyone except Lesley, who Mum had no idea I was seeing.

The same Christmas Dad had given me the snake necklace and bracelet, Mum gave Chloe a diary with a lock and a little key, which she kept hidden away or placed under the pillow on her bed on the nights when she slept in her own room. When Chloe opened her present on that Christmas Day, I can remember thinking the diary would be something else I'd need to check for any signs that he was doing anything to her. Keeping my little sister safe from him was something I thought about constantly, and as well as going through her school books to see if she'd written anything about him, I looked in her pants every night.

It wasn't just Chloe I monitored so carefully. I looked through Mum's things too – her letters and papers, even bank statements – because I had to know everything that was going on, so that I'd be prepared for ... I didn't really know what I had to be prepared for, I just knew I had to continue trying to protect Chloe, as I'd been doing since she was a baby and I'd discovered that there were things in our home that could harm us. I had spent many years of my childhood dreading whatever might be going to happen next, so maybe if I knew what it was before it happened, I reasoned, I could do something to pre-empt it.

During the couple of weeks after that Christmas, I had only been able to find the key and read Chloe's diary once, when I'd been reassured by the mundane things she'd written about school and going to the village shop with Mum. Even so, I knew she'd have been furious if she'd known what I'd done. I think the diary was in a drawer in her bedroom the second time I looked at it, towards the end of January. Or maybe it was the key that was in the drawer and the diary itself was under her pillow – I can't remember now. But, again, I was reassured by what she'd written, which was the sort of nonsense stuff you'd expect any 11-year-old child to write.

Chloe had glued some photographs on the two pages at the back of the diary, including one of her with her lovely long hair, holding a rabbit. When I noticed that the corner of one of the photos hadn't been stuck down properly, I lifted the edge and could see writing underneath it. I think I knew immediately that something was wrong and started pulling out the photos, unconcerned by the possibility that I might tear the pages.

I thought at the time that the words Chloe had written underneath the photos would be imprinted on my mind forever. But I can't really remember them now, except for one sentence, which said something like, 'When I was 8, 9 and 10 my dad made me kiss him and touch his willy.'

After I'd hidden the diary in my bedroom, I sat in the shower for two hours and sobbed. I'd been upset about many things during the last 11 years, but I'd never felt as heartbroken as I did that day. I just didn't know what to do. 'Why didn't I see it?' I kept asking myself. 'I was *looking* for it every day. How could I have missed it?'

A friend I confided in some time later asked why my mum hadn't realised what my dad was doing to me – in our house, almost right under her nose. But Mum hadn't been looking for it – I doubt whether she even knew there *were* men who abused their own children – whereas, with Chloe, I *had* been. And I had still missed it.

When I eventually came out of the shower, I phoned Lesley, who told me she'd meet me at Debbie's house as soon as I could get there. I had passed my driving test by that time and my granddad had helped me find me a good, roadworthy car, so I drove myself there, with the words 'How did I miss it?' swirling round and round in my head.

When I arrived at Debbie's house, Lesley was already there and I told them both what had happened.

'I'm afraid it's out of my hands now,' Lesley told me. 'Because of your sister's age, I'll have to report it to social services, and the police. You're going to have to tell your mum too, Heidi. Or I will, if you don't want to do it yourself. I'm sorry, but it's got to be done. You do understand that, don't you?'

My only thought when I'd phoned Lesley was that I needed to offload what I'd read in Chloe's diary. I hadn't had time to think about the fact that there would be consequences. 'I always thought it was just *my* secret,' I told her now. 'I thought it was going to die with me.'

Of course I was 'glad' that I'd found the diary, because it meant there wouldn't be any danger of Chloe being allowed to visit him anymore. But, at the same time, I couldn't help thinking, 'What have I done?' I suppose I was in a state of shock, which was exacerbated by the realisation that people I didn't know or trust, people who didn't love Chloe like I did, were going to control whatever happened next. It was a prospect that would have been daunting for anyone. For someone like me, who dreads not being in control of *any* situation, it was very frightening.

'You need to think about how you want to tell your mum,' Lesley advised me. 'I know it's going to be difficult for you, so I can give you two weeks to work through it and find a way to break the news to her. But if you haven't done it by then, I'm going to have to take action myself. I'm sorry, Heidi, but I'm sure you understand why.'

'Yes, I understand,' I said. 'Can I bring Mum to your office and tell her there?'

So that's what I did. Mum was doing the morning shift, and on the day I'd arranged with Lesley, I waited nervously for her outside the shop in town where she worked. I couldn't really afford the prawn sandwiches I'd bought for us, but I wanted to soften the blow of the horrendous thing I was about to tell her, and couldn't think of any way of doing it other than to buy something for her lunch I knew she'd like.

'I bought some sandwiches,' I told her when she came out of the shop, still wearing her uniform. 'I thought we could sit on that bit of green behind the cathedral to eat them. Then I need to take you somewhere and introduce you to someone.'

'Oh, right. Well, okay,' said Mum, crossing the road beside me without asking any questions.

After I'd taken just two bites of my sandwich I felt so sick I shoved it back in the bag and sat in anxious silence while Mum ate hers. Then we walked to the building a couple of streets away, where the charity now had its offices.

Lesley buzzed us up when I rang the bell, and when she greeted us at the top of the stairs, I told Mum, 'This is Lesley. She's been giving me counselling for a while now. The thing is …' I took a deep breath to try to stem the flow of tears that had started to spill out on to my cheeks. 'The thing is,' I said again, 'I've got something to tell you.'

'Okay,' Mum said, looking at me with an expression of bemused apprehension.

I could understand why she felt uneasy. Particularly for someone like my mum, who doesn't talk about anything personal or emotional, sitting there in a room with a total stranger, waiting to be told something obviously important but otherwise unimaginable, must have been very uncomfortable.

I had pictured in my head a million times what that moment would be like. Or, more accurately, the moment when I would tell my mum what had been happening to me. But I didn't think it would ever really come. And now that it had, what I was about to tell her was far worse than anything I'd ever imagined, because now it was about Chloe.

I tried several times to say the words I'd repeated over and over in my head during the last two weeks, but I couldn't get them out. Having pushed Mum away for so long, when all I really wanted was for her to hug me and tell me she loved me, it was even more difficult than I'd thought it was going to be to sit there, with tears streaming down my face, as she looked at me with a quizzical, slightly nervous expression, but no sign of any other emotion at all.

'Do you want to do this, Heidi?' Lesley asked me eventually. 'Or do you want me to tell your mum?'

'You do it.' It sounded more like a sob than words.

'Heidi was abused by your ex-husband from the age of seven until the age of thirteen,' Lesley said, turning her full attention to Mum. 'She has just read Chloe's diary, and from what Chloe has written in it, it is obvious that she was also abused by your ex-husband, between the ages of eight and ten.'

Lesley's tone was sympathetic and I imagine she was expecting – as I was – that my mum would be very upset by the news. But, after a very brief pause, all Mum said was, 'Oh, right. So what do we do now then?'

For a moment, Lesley was visibly taken aback. Then her expression became neutral again. For me, though, it was as if I'd been standing in a large, windowless room when someone casually flicked a switch and turned off all the lights, plunging me into total darkness before I'd had a chance to memorise the position of all the furniture I knew I would stumble into as I searched for the door.

This wasn't the way it was meant to be, and I hadn't ever felt as hurt or as unloved as I did at that moment. In fact, I don't think I could have felt any worse if Mum had actually said she didn't care about me or about the horrible things that had happened to me when I was a child. I realised later that her apparently cool, matter-of-fact response was probably at least partly due to shock. After all, how do you process information like that? At the time, however, it felt like a slap in the face.

'You need to report this to the police,' Lesley told Mum. 'I'll be beside you every step of the way, if that's what you want. But you need to make the phone call yourself.'

So Mum phoned the police and reported what she'd been told. Then she handed the phone to Lesley, who explained in more detail what had happened. Then, after an appointment had been made for Mum and me to go into the police station the following week to give our statements, we went home together on the bus. When we got there, Mum went upstairs and shut the door of her bedroom without a word and I went into my room and crawled under the bedcovers, where I stayed for the next three hours.

What hurt almost more than everything else that happened that day was seeing Mum hug Chloe when she got home from school. Their relationship, which had always been good, seemed to become even better from that day forward, as Mum cradled and supported Chloe in the way I had always longed for her to do for me.

Chloe asked me several times during the next few days if I'd seen her diary, and every time she asked me, I told her I hadn't. I could tell she didn't believe me, but there wasn't really anything she could do, particularly as she probably realised that it might arouse suspicion if she made too much fuss about something that, supposedly, contained just a few pages of childish notes along the lines of, 'Went to school today. Had fish fingers for tea.'

When the day came for Mum and me to give our statements to the police, Lesley went with us to a house in a town about 15 miles away, where I went first into a room that looked like a lounge except that there were several cameras on tripods. While I was in there, a woman spoke to me and explained what was going to happen. Then I was introduced to a really nice policeman called Dan who, unusually for me, I felt almost immediately I could trust.

We were there for ten hours that day. Lesley stayed with me the entire time, and Mum did too, although she didn't come into the room when I gave my statement. When we had a break for lunch, Lesley, Mum and I went to a cafe, where it soon became obvious that the relationship between the two of them was, mutually, very frosty, which made the atmosphere awkward. I think Mum felt Lesley was judging her for having apparently been oblivious to what was happening almost directly under her nose. And although I can understand why she might have felt that way, I don't think Lesley blamed her at all. What she might have found frustrating, however, was that, having got to know me so well during the months I'd been seeing her for counselling, she knew how desperately I wanted my mum's love and affection, which, even now, didn't seem to be forthcoming.

Because I felt that Mum had turned away from me in the one situation in which I *really* needed her, I was turning away too. Or, at least, I was withdrawing. I suppose that was a good thing in some ways, because it meant I was becoming stronger and more independent. It seemed to me at that time that if your mother can't say to you in a situation like that, 'I'm sorry for what happened to you and I understand now why you behaved the way you did,' then you have to consider the possibility that the problem in your relationship lies with her, not, as you have always believed, with you.

It took me another ten years to get to the point of being able to see things differently and to understand that, very often, my mother's reactions – or *non*-reactions – are more to do with her own issues than with the way she feels about me.

In the three weeks that passed between the day when I read Chloe's diary and the day I gave my statement to the police, I tried to talk to my sister too.

'I've seen your diary,' I told her eventually. 'I know something happened. Me and you are the same.' But she was angry – understandably – because I'd lied to her when she was searching so anxiously for it, and she resolutely refused to talk to me.

We made a plan with the police that Mum and I would pick Chloe up from school one day during the week after we'd given our statements and tell her, 'We're going somewhere. We'll explain when we get there.' In retrospect, I don't think it was the best way to handle things with 11-year-old Chloe and I think things like that are done differently today.

When we got to the house where the police were and explained to Chloe that she was going to be asked to make a statement about her dad, she locked herself in the toilet. It was a perfectly normal reaction in the circumstances. The problem was, the police didn't seem to have any protocol in place at that time to deal with a situation like that.

Looking back on it now, it must have been very damaging for Chloe to be taken out of school – somewhere she felt safe – and driven to a house she'd never seen before, where there were people who were all strangers to her but knew her secret about what her dad had done to her, who explained that what they wanted her to do was sit in front of a camera and tell them all about it. No wonder she refused to do it.

I think it was the policeman, Dan, who told me, 'You can take this to court, Heidi, but without Chloe's statement it will just be your word against his. It won't go anywhere. We *are* going to arrest your dad, but if Chloe won't speak, the case might never make it to court.'

So although I did feel very sorry for Chloe, I had huge anger for her too, because I felt so exposed. I had kept *my* secret for 11 years, from the age of 7 to 18, and I don't think I'd ever have told *anyone* about it except my counsellor Lesley if I hadn't discovered that he'd done the same to my little sister. So I suppose I felt resentful, too, because if Chloe *didn't* give her statement, I would have hurt all the people I loved for nothing.

The days between giving my statement to the police and my dad being arrested were tense and horrible. Mum and I had told Chloe that he mustn't know what had happened, and I was really anxious for my own sake, too, in case I bumped into him in the village or on a street somewhere in town. I was also very concerned about making sure I spoke to Tom before they arrested Dad, so that I could explain everything to him. Unfortunately, however, he heard the news from his father, and then wouldn't talk to me at all.

After Dad was arrested and charged, he wasn't allowed
to come within a certain distance of our house, so at least I
knew I was unlikely to walk out of the front door one morning and come face to face with him – although, knowing
him, that wasn't beyond the realms of possibility. Then, one
night, some friends decided I needed cheering up and persuaded me to go to a club in town with them. Dad's arrest
had been reported in the local paper, but it hadn't said what
the charges were, and I hadn't gone into details with any of
my friends, except to say that he wasn't allowed to have any
contact with us and that he wasn't the nice man everyone
thought he was.

The club we went to that night was the one I often
went to with friends, and we had been there for just a few
minutes when I saw him. I think he realised I was petri-
fied because he kept walking past where we were standing,
obviously trying – with some success – to intimidate me.
My friends huddled round me, forming a protective barrier
between us, but every time I looked up he was watching
me. I think he might have kept it up all evening – or at least
until we left the club – if one of my friends hadn't ended up
venting her anger and frustration by kicking him on the shin
as he strolled by, which finally took the smirk off his face.

My friends had meant well when they'd insisted on a
night out to try to take my mind off what had happened.
But seeing him there, leering at me across the dance floor in
the club, just seemed to underline the fact that everything
was a horrible mess. Having lived through one long nightmare as a child, I was now living through another. I hated

myself for not having protected Chloe the way I thought I'd been doing for the last few years. And now, because I believed that revealing the secret I'd been keeping since I was seven years old was the only way I could make sure she'd be safe from him in the future, it felt as though I had completely exposed myself. Chloe had barely spoken to me since the day I told her I'd read her diary. What was almost even worse than that, however, was that Tom wouldn't speak to me either, obviously because he didn't believe that what I'd said about his dad was true.

Chapter Six

Chloe

I've got friends who seem to be able to remember almost every detail of their childhood. But although I can visualise quite clearly the houses and the flat we lived in, I can't remember much about the abuse, when it started or how many times it happened. If there were more incidents than the few I can recall, I must have blocked them out.

Maybe it's because I still feel very angry about what happened when I was a child and I don't really want to remember anything. I know a lot of people believe that you *should* try to remember – I think my sister Heidi would be one of them. But my attitude is why contaminate the good life I've got now by poking around in the dark recesses of my subconscious mind and dredging up things I can't do anything about?

In fact, I'd more or less successfully blocked out *all* the bad things again until a few months ago, when Heidi said she wanted to write a book and asked me to tell my side of the story too. At first, I said I didn't want to. Then I realised when I thought about it a bit more that it was something I *had* to do, for Heidi's sake. I didn't want to read her part of the story, though. I thought it might help, in some ways, to understand why certain things happened the way they did. But it felt like dangerous ground, and I decided I'd rather wait until I thought I was ready to deal with it – if that time ever came.

There was always some invisible force driving Heidi on to work really hard, go to university and have a career; whereas the only thing I ever wanted was a family of my own. And I've got that now – a partner and three wonderful children I love, and a close relationship with my mum. But although I feel as if I've moved on with my life and don't have any need to go back and revisit the past, I know it's important to Heidi that this story is told so that she can draw a line underneath it.

Some people believe it's better to confront the bad things that have happened to you. In fact, someone said to me quite recently, 'If you don't deal with it now, it will come back to bite you one day, and when it does, you might get really depressed.' Maybe they are right. Maybe, if memories of all the bad things were swirling around in my head, affecting my day-to-day life and my ability to love and look after my children, I *would* need to confront them and try to deal with them. But I don't think that's the right thing for me – not now anyway. So I'm willing to take the chance.

I'm more like my brother Tom than Heidi in that respect: I think he and I both prefer not to deal with things until we have to. I'm probably worse than he is. It isn't that I don't care about stuff, it's just that if I can't change something, I don't see the point in making myself – and, by default, my family – unhappy by thinking about it. Shutting out worries and anxieties isn't always possible, of course. Which means that there are plenty of problems that have to be faced and dealt with, without actively trying to remember the ones I've forgotten about!

I'd probably feel differently about what happened to me as a child if he was still alive. But he's not, and it all seems like a very long time ago, although I know it really isn't and that what he did still has an effect on me in some ways today, and probably always will. Even if I can't consciously remember most of the horrible things, I know they must have played some part in moulding the adult I've become. They could be responsible for my lack of self-confidence, for example, and for how difficult I find it to trust people, even people I know well. But lots of people have 'issues' like that, and my attitude until now has been that as long as mine don't prevent me from leading a relatively normal life and doing all the things I need to do for my children and partner, I prefer not to go poking at the hornets' nest with a big stick.

I don't ever refer to him by the title he didn't do anything to earn, so I'm going to call him 'he' – in italics where it might otherwise be confusing. I can't really explain the reasons why I don't call him 'Dad' or 'my dad', except that it feels as though he stole the dad I should have had. And although I very rarely think about him at all, I *am* conscious of the fact that I envy my friends who have dads who walk them down the aisle when they get married and who are the first people they turn to whenever they need help or advice. Knowing that I won't ever have that relationship with anyone makes me resent him even more than I do because of what he did to me when I was a child. It's true that he stole my childhood. But because I don't have many memories of what he did, it's the fact that he 'stole' my father that really hurts.

Apparently, I was close to him when I was very young. I know Heidi thinks that he – and Mum – spoilt me and always gave me everything I wanted. She was seven years old when I was born, and maybe lots of older siblings feel like that when their parents continue to indulge the 'baby' of the family. Or maybe she's right and I was given more in some ways than she was. I don't remember enough about it to be able to make that judgement.

One of the few early memories I do have is of him taking me to his friend's house one day after I'd said I wanted a kitten, and telling me to choose one. That's how I got Rosy, who was tortoiseshell and one of the smallest kittens in the litter. I think Heidi was a bit jealous when he got Rosy for me, although not in a nasty way. But although she used to say that he always bought me whatever I wanted, Rosy is the only thing I can remember, and I don't think he actually *bought* her, because his friend was probably giving the kittens away.

Getting Rosy was one of the few happy memories I have of my childhood. Another is of Mum making me a velvet choker, which matched my dress and which I wore when she took me to a disco. I suppose there must have been a reason why I went with her to the disco, but I don't remember what it was, or what happened when we got there; I just remember wearing that choker and feeling very grown up.

I've got snippets of various other memories – bouncing on the bed on Christmas morning, for example, then going downstairs and seeing the bikes Father Christmas had brought for Heidi and Tom. I can't see *him* in that picture, or in any of the other mental images I have, such as the one of Mum, Heidi, Tom and me sitting round the table eating roast chicken for Sunday dinner. But I suppose he must have been there, some of the time anyway.

I do have an image of him sitting on the sofa in the living room, eating pistachio nuts out of a big bag that was on the floor beside him. I think it's a general rather than a specific memory, because it was something he used to do quite often, which possibly explains why, to this day, I can't bear to watch anyone eating pistachios.

I can also remember helping him to lay a patio in the back garden of our house, which must have been when I was about four – so maybe it isn't strictly accurate to say I 'helped him'. I think I just played with the clumps of muddy orange clay he was digging up and dumping in a wheelbarrow, which he then wheeled across the road and tipped over the hedge.

The next clear memory I have is of the night when I was six or seven years old and woke up to find him touching me under the duvet, moving his hands over my nipples and between my legs. I suppose it was fear that made me freeze and pretend to be asleep. Or maybe, because my mind couldn't process what was happening, it just stopped trying and shut down.

Most of the other images I can recall are fuzzy and out of focus: smells and the way I felt remind me of certain things, rather than any specific details of what happened. Another memory that *is* quite clear in my mind, however, is of sitting on the stairs with our dog, Lexi, one Sunday evening while Mum was in the kitchen and he was upstairs in the bathroom, having a shower. Mum was cooking roast chicken and it was dark outside – it must have been in the winter, as we always ate our dinner at six o'clock, and I know it was a Sunday, because that was the only day we had chicken. I was pretending to be foraging for food and kept sneaking into the kitchen when Mum's back was turned and stealing bits of meat, which I shared with Lexi.

The first time I heard him call my name, I put my arms around Lexi's neck and pressed my face against her fur, which smelt doggy and chickeny at the same time. I heard him shout 'Chloe' again, impatiently this time, and then angrily when I still didn't answer. Bad things must have happened before that day, because I somehow knew I was only delaying the inevitable. So, eventually, I unclasped my hands from around Lexi's neck and stood up, giving her a little push that sent her scuttling down the stairs as I turned and walked slowly up them.

I can remember standing in the doorway of his and Mum's bedroom, not wanting to step inside. He was by the window, with a towel wrapped round his waist, and he told me to come in and sit on the bed. Then he turned off the light and lay down beside me, and although he didn't close the bedroom door, the room was quite dark because the landing light was off too.

I was just sitting there, frozen to the spot, when he said, almost casually, 'Let's have a kiss.' When I turned to face him, he was pointing to his mouth. So I kissed him on the lips and was turning away again when he put his hand on the back of my head and said, 'Keep going, all the way down.' Then he unwrapped the towel, pushed my head down towards his penis and told me to kiss it. He smelt of soap and his skin was warm and damp, although not in a nice way, and I can remember feeling embarrassed and dirty, for reasons I didn't understand.

When Mum called up the stairs, 'Dinner's ready,' I sat up so quickly I almost toppled backwards and fell off the bed. I don't know how long we'd been in the bedroom – it was probably just a few minutes, but it seemed much longer.

The next thing I remember, I was sitting at the dinner table, and that's where the memory ends. I don't know whether Heidi and Tom were there or if I ate my dinner – I suppose those details were insignificant in comparison to what had just happened, even though I didn't have any understanding at all of what *had* happened, upstairs, on *his* bed.

Another time, Mum was in the kitchen and I was in the lounge with him, watching *Thunderbirds* on TV. Again, I don't know where Heidi and Tom were; they would both have been in their teens, so they were probably out. *He* was eating pistachio nuts, snapping their shells open, then dropping the two empty halves onto a small table at the side of the sofa before flicking the nut into his mouth. I think I was so intent on the programme we were watching, I wasn't consciously aware of anything else he might have been doing until he patted his knee with his hand and said, 'Why don't you come and sit on my lap?'

Although it sounded like a question, I knew it wasn't, and that saying 'No' wasn't an option. So I got up from the chair I was sitting in and when I sat down again, on his lap, he turned me round so that I was facing him, took hold of my right hand, placed it on his jeans and started rubbing it over his penis. I could feel my cheeks burning with embarrassment and although my arm was rigid, he just kept moving my hand up and down until his penis was erect. Then he unzipped his jeans, placed my hand directly on it and continued to do the same thing, while I looked over his shoulder at the sunshine that was streaming in through the window behind him.

Some time later – I don't know what age I was, but it was the last event I can recall – I was alone with him in the house when he started play-fighting with me and pinching my nipples through the thin top I was wearing. It was something he often did, in a jokey way, when he was messing about, so it was like a normal thing. But although I laughed when he tickled me, I have always hated being tickled and I tried to fend him off, which was pointless really, as he was much stronger than me. Then, after a while, he picked me up, dumped me on the sofa, pulled my top up and started blowing raspberries on my tummy. And suddenly I felt sick, because I knew what was coming – or, at least, I knew his play-fighting was about to turn into something different.

When he pulled down my trousers and started blowing raspberries on the exposed skin, I kept saying, 'No! No, please, stop it.' But he didn't take any notice as he put his fingers inside me, then his tongue, while I lay there, numbed by shock and barely able to breathe.

I don't know what happened after that. Trying to remember is like looking at a series of photographs with all the details of the images blanked out. I do remember the smells, though – of Brut aftershave, beer and cigars. They are smells that still stop me dead in my tracks today and make me feel physically sick.

As I got older, I always felt panicky in his company. Whenever I was alone with him in his van, I would be on edge all the time, wondering where we were really going and afraid in case something happened. But he never did anything to me outside the house – at least, not as far as I can remember.

I wasn't frightened of him when I was a young child. The fear came later. But I *was* embarrassed. Not *by* him exactly, but by being *with* him. I suppose it was because the things he did to me made our relationship uncomfortable and uncertain. The relationship a young child has with his or her parents should be natural and uncomplicated. That's what it was like with Mum. So although I don't think I knew that the things he did to me were wrong – in fact, I don't think I ever questioned or even thought about them at the time – I always felt uneasy when I was with him. Embarrassed isn't really the right word, but it's the only one I can think of to describe the feeling I always had of wishing the ground would open and swallow me up.

I felt shocked, too, by what he did, even when I didn't understand it. It was as if he was sucking the life out of me and I was completely powerless to do anything to stop him. Even now, I find it very difficult to deal with people invading my personal space. I hug my family and I cuddle my children all the time, but I'm not a naturally cuddly-huggy person. If someone gets too close to me – physically, I mean – I have to bite my tongue to stop myself saying, 'You need to take a step back and move away from me.' I don't even hug my closest friends – I just can't do it. It feels . . . unnatural, that's the word. And that's how I felt whenever I was with him as a child: that our relationship was somehow unnatural.

He was well aware of the fact that I didn't want to do the things he made me do when I was a little girl, even though I didn't know at the time that they weren't normal. And he didn't make a big deal out of hiding what he did. Although he said it was 'our secret', I don't remember him ever saying explicitly not to tell Mum about it. He wasn't ever aggressive towards me. His attitude wasn't 'You *will* do this.' It was more, 'Well, this is what we do.' So I think I simply accepted that it was what everyone did, and that the way I felt about it was just 'my problem'.

I don't think what he did to me was an everyday occurrence. It was probably more opportunistic – something that happened whenever he thought he could get away with it. And he *did* get away with it, even when Mum was in the kitchen or there were other people in the house. Perhaps that was part of the thrill for him, knowing he could be found out.

The house we were living in when he and Mum divorced had a big bedroom at the front, a medium-sized room in the middle, which was where Heidi and I slept until the really serious trouble started between our parents, and a small room at the back, which was Tom's. That all got changed around before they divorced though, when he moved into our room and Heidi and I slept in with Mum.

Some of the most frightening things that happened during my childhood took place in the bedrooms of that house, when I was pretending to be asleep. The night he came into my room and touched me was the first time I remember anything like that happening. But there were other frightening things too, like all the times he woke Mum up and started swearing and spitting at her, telling her he was going to cut little Lexi into pieces and bury her in the garden, then set the house on fire with us inside it. He was always drunk when he said things like that to Mum, and I was always very scared – because I thought he might really hurt her and because I believed that, one night when we were all asleep, he would carry out his threat and we'd all be burned to death. In fact, the fear that he would kill us stayed with me for many years.

You might think I'd have felt safer after Heidi and I
moved into their bedroom and he moved into ours, but it
was very frightening to wake up in the middle of the night
as I sometimes did and see him leaning over Mum saying
horrible things to her – that she was a whore, for example,
and that he knew she was seeing someone else. He always
said those things in an aggressive whisper, because he didn't
want to wake us up, I suppose. But I think I was more afraid
on those occasions than I would have been if he'd been
shouting at her.

In the period just before they got divorced and he moved
out, he used the middle bedroom as his sitting room too.
He had a phone in there, and it's where he used to spend
most of his time when he was at home, filling it with smoke
and the stench of alcohol. I don't remember him doing anything to me during that time, but I don't know for sure.

One day, Mum told us we might be moving out of
that house and going to live in another town, but in
the end, *he* left instead, which would have been fine if
Tom hadn't gone with him. I cried myself to sleep for
nights after my brother left. I know I went to the flat
they shared on at least one occasion, because I remember that they had two terrapins in a tank, which smelled
really bad, and Tom let me help him clean it out and
feed them. I think that memory has stuck in my mind
because I missed Tom so much, and because I really enjoyed helping him that day.

I can't work out how old I was when *he* and Mum
split up. What is very clear in my mind, however, is how

much better everything was when he wasn't living with us anymore, bullying and shouting at Mum, and frightening me. The only thing that was bad about it was that Tom wasn't there.

Then I was given a diary for Christmas, and a few weeks later, everything suddenly became far worse than it had ever been.

Chapter Seven

Chloe

I have problems with dates and with trying to remember what age I would have been when certain things happened. For some reason, my brain won't let me access that sort of information and I tend to think I was much older than I probably was when particular events occurred. But I can't have been more than ten when he took me to a fireworks display one evening. It was certainly after the divorce, and after he'd moved out with Tom. I don't think anything happened that night, so the reason it sticks in my mind is probably because he met up with a woman there who he obviously knew well and who had kids, which bothered me, because of what he'd done to me.

It might have been Christmas that same year when he came to the house with Tom to give Heidi and me our presents – a toy pig for Heidi and a blow-up chair and a diary for me. The diary had a lock and a little key, and I remember Heidi saying, 'You can write all the things you don't want anyone else to know in there.' In fact, that's all I remember of that day, except that it felt awkward him being in the house and that although I was happy because Tom had come with him, I kept wishing *he* would go.

About a month later, my diary disappeared. I told Mum and Heidi several times that I'd lost it, and they both said they hadn't seen it and didn't know where it was. But I didn't trust Heidi and I was certain she'd taken it. I really hoped she hadn't though, because as well as writing things like 'Went to school' and sticking photos on some of the pages, I'd written a story at the back of the diary that I didn't want her – or anyone else – to see.

I'd written the secret story on the page inside the back cover and the one adjoining it. Part of it was a sort of love story, about a girl falling in love with a man. Except that the two characters in it were actually *him* and me, and some of it was true. The fact that the man I wrote about – at the age of 11 – was my dad is a testament to how confused I was. He hadn't done anything to me since I'd been given the diary for Christmas, so I didn't write anything about him on the pages with the dates on them. What I wrote at the back, however, was that we had had sex, which actually wasn't true.

I can remember panicking and trying to scrape off the words as soon as I'd written them. And when that didn't work, I stuck photographs over them – one of Lexi, I think, another of Mum and another of me with some kittens or rabbits. Then I locked the diary, put it under my pillow and hid the key.

I didn't know why Heidi looked under the photographs, or why she took my diary in the first place. Obviously, I didn't do as good a job as I thought I'd done of hiding the diary itself, the key or the words. And, being the sort of person she is, I know that once Heidi realised there was something written there, she wouldn't have been able to rest until she'd read it. She had good reason to be suspicious on this occasion, of course, although I didn't know that at the time.

I must have been looking for the diary for a few days by the time Heidi admitted, 'I found it. I told Mum and we know what's happened. We need to tell the police. But *he* mustn't know that we know, so you've got to act normal around him. You can't say anything to *anyone*, not even Tom.'

I felt shocked by what she'd done and mortified when I thought about what she'd read. But I think my overwhelming emotion at the time – and for a long time afterwards – was anger. Not only had she taken *my* locked diary from underneath *my* pillow and read it, she had then gone behind my back and shown it to Mum.

Heidi had always mothered me, but this was something different: she had interfered in something that was supposed to be private, and now she was *telling* me what was going to happen. I hated the fact that I had no say in any part of it, not least because it made me feel the way I used to feel when *he* was doing things to me – frozen and totally helpless. I think I shouted at her when she told me she'd 'found' my diary. Then I ran upstairs, threw myself on my bed and sobbed hot tears of shame and embarrassment.

When the initial shock started to subside, I began to hate her for what she'd done. All that time I'd been searching with increasing desperation for the diary, thinking I must have misplaced it – although I couldn't understand how that could have happened – she had told me, 'I don't know where it is, Chloe. No, I haven't seen it. I didn't touch it.' But she'd been lying. And when I found out what she'd done, it felt as though the good relationship we'd always had and all the sisterly feelings I'd felt for her had been re-placed by anger, distrust and, for a while, hatred.

I think I'd known all along that, despite her assurances, Heidi *did* have my diary. There wasn't really any other ex-planation for its disappearance. To this day, though, I still don't understand why she didn't come to me first when she read it. If she'd told me what he'd done to *her*, I think I would have told her that it was happening to me too. Then we could have gone to Mum *together*.

I hated the fact that Heidi had stolen my most secret thoughts, and that, without saying anything to me, she had then told Mum about them. What I hated even more, how-ever, was knowing they had both been talking about me behind my back and planning what they were going to do.

For a while, life just seemed to go on as normal, except that now our 'normal loving family' had a huge secret that involved me, but that I didn't have any say in, because I was just a child and my voice didn't need to be heard. Nobody spoke about what had happened, and nobody wanted to know what I thought or if I had any feelings or opinions about any of it.

About eight years ago, I started working at a nursery that was on the same road as a large brick building, which is a sort of warehouse, and as I walked past it one morning on my way to work, a memory suddenly popped into my head of going there with him when I was a little girl. I'd forgotten until that moment that he had a workshop in that building, which was almost like a massive shed, full of the equipment he used when he sang in pubs and clubs, as well as all sorts of tools and other items I can't remember now. What I do still remember very clearly, however, is the smell of damp wood and cigarette smoke.

I couldn't work out that day when I walked past it why I had such a bad feeling about that building, because I know nothing happened there – I'm certain of that. Then I remembered that he'd taken me there one day over the weekend before he was going to be arrested, when Mum and Heidi had told me that I must 'act normal'. It was an instruction I don't think any child would have found easy to follow under any circumstances, and because I didn't want to stay in the workshop with him, I decided to walk to the village shop and buy some sweets. Then he drove me back to Mum's. It was all a non-event really, but I must have remembered it because of how anxious I felt at the time.

I didn't ever get my diary back. I did see it again some years later, in one of my mum's drawers, and all the feelings of shame and embarrassment came flooding back, as though I was living the nightmare all over again. But the next time I looked it had gone, and I still don't know to this day what happened to it.

At the time, it was almost as if Heidi's actions had put her on the same level as *him*, making me do things I didn't want to do and snatching away even the small amount of control I'd thought I had over my own life. She never asked me if I *wanted* to speak to a policeman, for example; she just *told* me one day that that's what we were going to do.

We went to this place that was like a cross between a family bungalow and a police station, where we sat in tub chairs in a room that was cold and unwelcoming, despite the pictures on the walls and vases of flowers on the tables. I didn't want to go there. I didn't want to be there. I didn't want people to talk to me. And I certainly didn't want to talk to *anyone* about the incredibly embarrassing things I'd written in my diary or about the things *he* had done and made me do.

After we'd waited for a while in that room, I can remember walking down a corridor and into another room where there was a round table, two chairs and a bed. I sometimes wonder if I only imagined that there was a bed in there, but I know I didn't, because I can still remember vividly how sick I felt and that I was freaking out, thinking, 'What are they going to make me do?' Then, when I saw the video cameras, I burst into tears, ran out of the room and locked myself in the toilet.

I felt humiliated and belittled by everything that had happened, and I was very resentful towards Heidi for being, in my mind, entirely responsible for it all. This time, however, I *did* have some control, and it didn't matter how much she tried to cajole and encourage me, or how angry she got with me, I held out and refused to talk to anyone.

I didn't like *him* by that time, mostly because of the things I'd heard him say to Mum and the way he'd treated her before he left. So it wasn't that I was refusing to talk about what he'd done to me because it would have felt like treachery. It was just that I was too embarrassed to say anything to anyone, let alone to total strangers in a room in someone else's house where there were video cameras and a bed!

Heidi wasn't giving up that easily, though. She'd already given her statement by the time I was taken to that house and she told me, 'They need your evidence before they can press charges.' So then, added to all the other distressing and confusing emotions, I felt as though a huge responsibility I didn't understand was resting entirely on my shoulders, and that it would be all my fault if whatever it was that everyone wanted to happen, didn't.

Mum didn't put any pressure on me about it, but it felt as though Heidi really did. It's only when I think about it now that I realise her determination to see him charged for what he'd done to us both might have been partly due to the fact that she thought she'd failed to protect me from him. I didn't understand any of that at the time though; it just felt like she was doing what he'd done – taking control and not giving me any opportunity to say 'No!'

'If I *do* talk to them, I don't want you to see it on the video,' I told Mum and Heidi. 'I don't want you to hear what I'm saying.'

'No. No, we won't,' they assured me. But I didn't trust Heidi anymore, and there was no way I was going to go back into that room and say anything she might be able to hear. So I cried and told Mum I didn't want to do it, I just wanted to go home.

'It's all right. Don't worry, Chloe,' Mum said. 'You don't have to do it if you don't want to. You can just—'

'She *needs* to do this, Mum,' Heidi interrupted her. But I was way beyond persuading by that time and wild horses couldn't have dragged me back into that room, which was like something out of a nightmare – or like that film *The Cat in the Hat*, where everything's weird and chaotic.

I think we went back into the room with the tub chairs after I eventually came out of the toilet, and Heidi tried to persuade me again, saying, 'You *must* do it, Chlo. You don't want him to be let off and then do the same thing to someone else, do you?' Which made me feel even worse, although I still insisted through my tears, 'I *can't*.'

Eventually, the woman who was with us – who I think must have been a police liaison officer – said, 'It's all right, Chloe. You don't have to do it now. You can come back and do it another time.'

Then, suddenly, everything changed again. Not because of anything that happened – at least, not anything that I was aware of – but because, after all the tears and anger and build-up to *him* being arrested, nothing happened at all.

Chapter Eight

Tom

Everything was 100 per cent all right until I was 15. We were a normal family. My parents argued, and Heidi had a lot of rows with my dad when we were in our teens. But that's what normal families do, isn't it?

There were some arguments I didn't understand, like the one my dad had with Heidi when she wouldn't let him sleep in Mum's bed. But I can't recall anything else that struck me as particularly strange during that period. I don't remember Dad moving into the middle bedroom either. Although I do remember before that, when I was about 10 or 11, Heidi and I used to sit at the top of the stairs when they got back from the pub on a Saturday night, listening to them shouting at each other. I expect all kids get that horrible feeling in the pit of their stomachs when their parents argue. But I was so focused on school and doing stuff with my friends that although I didn't like it when they rowed, it didn't really worry me unduly.

Then they got divorced, and that was that.

Mum told me, 'Heidi and Chloe are staying here with me, and you know I'm happy for you to do that too. But it's your choice.' I think I had a day to decide. And I can remember thinking, 'If I stay with Mum, she won't be strict enough with me.' Even at that age, I knew I needed someone to set and enforce boundaries that would stop me going the wrong way. So that was the rationale for my decision to go with my dad. That and the fact that I felt sorry for him. Staying with Mum and my sisters would have made me feel as though *I* was the one splitting the family up and sending him out in the rain on his own. Needing boundaries was the reason I gave Mum, though. To which she responded, calmly, 'Okay. But you know you are always welcome here.'

I wasn't really naughty as a kid – I suppose I was just a bit silly, and sometimes did things without thinking about the consequences. For example, when I was about 13, a couple of older lads who lived in the village gave me some cannabis and got me totally stoned. I came back to the house just as Dad was going out, and by the time he got to the pub, these lads were already there, laughing and joking to everyone about what they'd done.

I was asleep – and still really stoned – when my dad got back from the pub, came into my room, turned the light on and really kicked off. He ended up phoning the police at about three o'clock in the morning because he wanted them to give me a talking to. They weren't interested though, and told him, 'Look, we're not sending someone out at this time of night. There's nothing we can do anyway.' But he was a very persuasive, stubborn man, and when he insisted, 'You are sending someone out to the house *now* to explain to my son why he shouldn't be smoking cannabis. That's what you're there for,' they sent two officers in a car.

'This really isn't a good start for you,' one of the police officers told me. 'How do you think it affects your family?' But I don't think I was capable of rational thought at all at that moment. After they'd gone, my dad grounded me for two months. And just to prove that I didn't care, I sat on a piece of spare ground opposite the house the first time I was allowed out again and smoked the last little bit of weed I'd saved from that night.

Dad drank a lot, every weekend. So I don't think he *really* cared about the fact that I'd smoked cannabis. It was just a control thing, because he'd been embarrassed by everyone at the pub laughing when the two guys joked about how stoned I was.

I wasn't frightened of him as a kid. He'd give me a smack if I misbehaved, and I definitely felt that I had to obey him, but he didn't ever punch me or anything like that. I loved him. That's what makes all this even weirder. I thought he was a good dad – apart from getting drunk every weekend and shouting at Mum. So it's been really hard trying to analyse what he did and to think of reasons why he did it.

I still don't understand it, of course – I don't suppose anyone does. Probably one of the main effects it's had on me is to make me paranoid as a parent. Because of what he did, my partner and I never leave our children with anyone else, and one of the reasons we chose the nursery they go to is because everyone who works there is a woman. I know that's oversimplifying things, and it happens with women too, but if I can't literally wrap the kids in cotton wool and make sure they have no interactions with anyone when I'm not there, I can at least ensure that they don't come into contact with men like my dad.

While I loved and trusted him throughout my entire childhood, Heidi and Chloe were learning from an early age that he wasn't the man I thought he was. So why didn't *I* know? Why did I believe he was someone completely different? Why didn't I pick up on *something* when he was abusing my sisters in the house I was living in with them? It's hard to get my head round questions like that, and I know they won't ever be answered now.

I was 14, or maybe 15, when I left home with him and we moved, temporarily, into a hostel in a nearby town. It was a horrible place. The flat we lived in had a living room with a kitchen area, a TV and bed in it, which is where my dad slept, and a bedroom, which I had. There was also a shower room, which we shared with whoever was living in the room next door. The housing estate the hostel was on was rough and depressing too. Looking back, it might have been better if he'd left me at home until he had somewhere decent – or at least less squalid – to live.

We must have been living in the hostel for about six or seven months – I know we were there over Christmas – and I hated it. I had a two-mile walk to school every morning, and a two-mile walk back again every afternoon, through the estate, which would have been okay in the summer, but it was a dark, miserable trek in the winter, when we were there.

Dad was quite disorganised and didn't make any effort in terms of cooking or trying to make the place more like a home. We ate pizzas mostly, or other types of takeaway food. I used to think he was grateful that I'd gone with him. I wonder now, though, if the real reason he wanted me there was because it meant he'd be rehoused more quickly than he would have been if he was on his own. I helped him with his gigs too – I suppose I was quite handy to have around for practical reasons like that.

We were still living in the hostel when I got a job through a friend cleaning council offices in the evenings after school. You had to be 18 to do it, which was a potential hurdle that was easily overcome by applying some Tipp-Ex to my birth certificate, adding a new date of birth, then photocopying it. The reason I wanted that job particularly was because the pay was good for someone who was still at school. I worked there with a couple of other lads my age for four or five months, until one of them got fired and retaliated by giving the game away and getting me, the other friend and the boss fired too.

I got a girlfriend around the same time as I got that job. So every day became the same cycle of walking to school, doing my job, going to see my girlfriend, Fran, going home, eating the meal he always cooked, going to bed, going to school … Then, at the weekends, I'd work with him.

Fran lived with her parents and although I'd sometimes stay over at her house, I never took her back to our place, even after we moved out of the hostel and into a two-bedroom flat, which was equally minging – the only furniture in the place was a heater, a microwave, a rough old sofa and a bed that was given to me by a neighbour. There were no carpets – just bare concrete floors that made the cold rooms even colder. But at least it was better than where we *had* been living, and my bedroom had a door I could shut when I wanted some privacy.

I didn't tell anyone how much I hated living in the hostel and then that flat. Heidi and I used to argue about everything during that period, and although I didn't really know what she meant when she told me before I left home with him, 'You'll be back soon,' the fact that she apparently believed I would be, made me determined not to go home.

Even when I was 15 and 16, I used to go out drinking with him every week, at a club where they sold drinks for £1 on Monday nights. Then I'd get up the next morning and go to school. I'd stopped focusing on my schoolwork by that time – it's difficult to concentrate in the classroom when you've got a hangover! No one at school knew I was drinking though. My parents didn't socialise with other parents, so if I didn't tell my friends what was going on, they had no other way of knowing.

On Saturdays, I'd help Dad with his gardening job, and on Sundays we'd set up his PA equipment at banger races or stock-car events. He was impulsive and never had a plan of action, and didn't ever do any job that involved having to work for other people. He just worked at weekends, so that he had weekdays free to do whatever he wanted, which mostly revolved around converting what he'd earned into 'liquid assets' and drinking them.

When I finished school at 16, I went to college for just one day before deciding that I wanted money more than an education. Mum wasn't very happy with my decision, but Dad was okay about it. 'It's up to you,' he told me – after I'd decided to get a job. 'You have to make your own decisions, because you're the one who'll have to stand by them.' In retrospect, I think his reaction was more about him than what was best for me, because he wanted me to be free to work with him at weekends.

I got a job cleaning toilets – for the council again – mostly in a nearby seaside town, although basically wherever and whenever they needed me. It was horrendous work, which I did from anything between two and five days a week. But it was good money for a 16-year-old just out of school.

Dad didn't really care about money. I kept what I earned cleaning toilets and he gave me a fiver a day for helping him at the weekends, which seemed fair, as we were living on the money he earned. When he'd paid the bills and for any other essentials that had to be bought and paid for, he'd say, 'I've got this much left. Shall we go out and spend it?' He just wanted to have a good time. In fact, he was quite selfish in that respect, and didn't ever think long term: if he had money, he spent it, and tomorrow would look after itself.

I was the same until I was about 26 – I used to spend every penny I earned on having a good time, just like he did. I was earning good money in my twenties, working in sales, and I could easily spend £2,000, even £3,000, over two or three weekends. I don't do it now, though. Now I've got a family and I want a steady income so that I can support them. I think that's what Heidi and Chloe want too – to be part of a normal, average family with 2.4 children.

It wasn't really a father/son relationship we had when I was in my teens. We were more like mates hanging out together. I was well able to look after myself, so he let me get on with it and do my own thing. That probably contributed towards the distance that began to develop between us, when I started spending more and more time at my girlfriend's house.

There aren't any excuses for what he did. Whatever experiences you have as a kid, you can make a choice about what sort of adult you become. I do think there was something bad in his background though, and that his dad was probably quite physical with him when he was a child, although as a granddad he was great with us kids.

I always thought Dad's brother George had the potential to be quite a violent person. In fact, I've got a vague memory of him threatening to bottle my dad on one occasion. That isn't something I would ever do, whatever the circumstances, so I think there must be some reason why you'd have that mentality. Dad had it too, and often used to tell me, 'It doesn't matter who the kid is. Even if he's the biggest kid in school, you don't ever back down. You fight.' He didn't ever talk about his background, though. We didn't really *talk* about anything. It was all just banter – light-hearted stuff – rather than real conversations.

What he *was* good at was fixing things and finding solutions to practical problems. If someone's car had broken down and no one else could repair it, he'd just keep working on it until he got it running again. He often did that sort of thing for friends – I think it was part of his need to be liked by people, rather than because he particularly cared about helping them.

Something I discovered about him when we lived together during that period was that he was actually very paranoid. 'You can't trust anyone,' he used to tell me. 'Their intentions are usually quite different from what you think they are.' He always thought there was some undisclosed, underlying reason for everything people said and did. And he was very convincing – I suppose because he really believed it himself. It took me a long time to realise it isn't true.

Even the simplest, most innocuous statement could set him off. I remember a man in a fishing tackle shop saying to him one day, 'Ah, are you playing away from home today?' The man had been a friend of his for a long time and it was just one of those things people say that don't really mean anything. My dad's way of dealing with situations that made him paranoid was by being flamboyant and acting like he was everyone's best friend. So he laughed and joked with the man in the fishing tackle shop. But his attitude changed completely as soon as we stepped outside and he kept asking me, 'What did he mean by "playing away from home"? You can't trust that man.' He'd often say the same sort of thing about someone he'd just been exchanging friendly banter with, and even if you provided him with any amount of cast-iron proof to the contrary, it wouldn't make any difference.

He always appeared to be very confident – to people who didn't know him like I did – and a lot of people liked him. Not Mum's parents, though. Although, come to think of it, I don't *know* that was the case, it was actually the things *he* said about *them* that made me believe it was. But that might just have been his paranoia speaking. It did make me like my granddad less, however, because I can remember thinking, 'If he doesn't like my dad, he doesn't like me.'

Dad's paranoia included Mum too, and before they divorced he was always accusing her of cheating on him. In fact, it was the cause of almost all their arguments – him saying she'd given someone the eye in the pub and insisting it meant she wanted to sleep with them.

He had a few girlfriends when he was single again. Sometimes, he'd bring a woman back from the club and I'd go and spend the night at Fran's house. Nothing lasted very long though, and I never got involved.

Then everything changed. Or, at least, something happened that blew a hole in our relationship and made me question everything I thought I knew about my dad.

Chapter Nine

Tom

My mobile rang early one morning after I'd stayed the night at my girlfriend's house. As soon as I answered it, Dad shouted at me, 'Did you know about this? You knew, didn't you? That's why you're staying over there.'

'Dad, I stay here all the time,' I said, when I could get a word in. 'In fact, I'm more likely to be here than at home. What is it? What's happened?'

'You knew, didn't you? I know you did,' he persisted. 'Heidi's made allegations. The police came and took me to the police station in a van. I'll tell you when I pick you up. I'm leaving now.'

Mum rang almost as soon as I'd put down the phone and asked if I'd spoken to Heidi or Dad. 'I'm just going to meet him,' I told her. 'I don't know what's happened, but I'll phone you later.' I don't think I did call her back that day, though.

I was waiting about half a mile up the road from Fran's house when he arrived and we drove a short distance to a lay-by, where he cut the engine and demanded again, 'Did you know about this?'

'About *what*, Dad?' I asked.

'Heidi's made these allegations about me. I know she hates me but I don't know why she'd do this. It makes no sense – going to these extremes just because she's annoyed with me about something.'

'I don't understand,' I told him. 'What kind of allegations has Heidi made?'

'She's accused me of doing things to her,' he said. He didn't explain what the 'things' were, but I guessed, roughly, what he meant and I was massively shocked. 'She *must* have made it up,' I thought. 'I was there. I lived in the same house. I would have seen something. I would have known if something like that had been going on.' At the time, it just seemed crazy. Now, however, with the benefit of hindsight, it did explain why Heidi hated him the way she did.

Looking back on it now, I should have put two and two together, but the truth didn't even cross my mind at the time. Things were different even just a few years ago, and most people had no idea that there are apparently normal men who sexually abuse their children. In fact, when I used to insist on using the men's toilets when we went to the supermarket as kids, Mum would ask the RAC man who had a stall outside to take me in. Fortunately, he was a nice man, but that isn't something anyone in their right mind would do today. So, as I say, there didn't seem to me to be any possibility that the accusations Heidi had apparently made against Dad were true. What seemed far more likely, as he said, was that she'd made them because she hated him for some other reason of her own.

For the next half an hour, we sat in his van in the lay-by while I tried to convince him I hadn't known anything about it. I swore that I hadn't spoken to Heidi, Mum or Chloe for at least a couple of days. Then I told him every single thing I'd done the previous day and the day before it, so he'd realise that staying over at my girlfriend's house for the night hadn't been pre-planned to avoid being at home when the police came for him.

Eventually, he said he was hungry, so we went to a cafe to have some breakfast. He didn't mention it again – not for a few days anyway – and for a while life returned to (almost) normal. For me, though, the questioning had only just started, because now I had to try to work out what the truth of it all might be and where I sat on the whole did he/didn't he issue.

I knew Heidi had a lot of anger inside her – a fact she'd illustrated very clearly when I took a steel toecap to the balls during one of our fights! I suppose the truth is that we both had a lot of anger inside us, and we could clash over almost anything. A disagreement about whether one of us had picked up the other's pen, for example, could end in a full-on physical fight, but only after the divorce, during the brief period before I left home to live with our dad. We were good friends before that, when we were growing up, and neither of us is at all aggressive by nature. I realise now that it must have felt to Heidi as though I wasn't there for her. She must have been very hurt when I went off to live with Dad after what he'd done to her, even though I didn't know anything about it until the day he was picked up by the police.

Heidi went round to Fran's house to try to talk to me before Dad did that same morning, but she arrived just after I'd left. So she told my girlfriend and her family everything instead, which annoyed me at the time, particularly because Fran's brother was a friend of mine and I really didn't want him, or anyone else, to know about it. It didn't make any sense to me either, because it felt almost as though her telling them was a win for her dad. But maybe that was just because I didn't know who to believe at that point and I hadn't yet got my head round what it all meant, or what it must have cost Heidi emotionally during all those years when she had kept his secret. Perhaps she hadn't intended to tell anyone else, but when Fran opened the door and Heidi burst into tears, they asked her in, because they were a really nice, loving family, and I suppose, having psyched herself up to tell *me*, she felt as though she needed to tell *someone*.

I'd always admired my dad for being able to talk to and get on with anyone. His friends always said how honest and what a great guy he was, and that there wasn't anything he couldn't do if he put his mind to it. I was used to hearing only positive things about him, which must have added to all the other reasons there seemed to be for making him my role model when I was a boy.

The question I kept asking myself was why, if what Heidi said was true, I hadn't seen anything suspicious myself. After all, it wasn't as though I'd been sent away to boarding school. I'd been there, at home, all the time until I was 15, Heidi was 17 and Chloe was 10.

I still hadn't been able to work out what or who to believe when my dad made me his messenger. First, though, he persuaded me and a friend of his to sign a document. I can't remember actually signing my name to it, or even what it said, except that it was something about Heidi having tried to poison him by putting cleaning chemicals in his coffee while we were still living at home. 'Go and see her,' he told me, 'and tell her that if she doesn't withdraw her accusations against me, I'll file charges against *her*.'

At first, I refused to have any part in it. Heidi and I hadn't been getting on for some time, but she was still my sister and the whole thing just felt weird and wrong. But Dad kept going on and on about it, insisting that if I didn't do what he was asking me to do, he would be going to prison for a very long time for crimes he hadn't committed.

In the end, I gave in to the unrelenting pressure he was exerting on me and went round to Mum's house one day to tell Heidi the story he had told me to tell her. He hadn't gone into any great detail when he primed me. 'Just tell her you know she's lying,' he said again. 'And that if she doesn't drop the charges, I'm going to tell the police she tried to kill me.' So that's what I did.

Thinking about it now, I wonder if maybe I didn't actually sign a document at all. Maybe I just told her I'd seen one that was part of the evidence he was gathering together to prove she'd tried to poison him – I can't remember. Heidi didn't care anyway. She just laughed and said, 'Tell him he can do what he wants.'

Then I was even more confused, and still didn't know who to believe. What didn't help was the fact that I did believe Heidi *could* have done what Dad was accusing her of doing – because she was always so angry with him and obviously hated him – but I didn't actually believe that she *did* do it.

I don't know when he was charged, but things really kicked off after his arrest was reported in the local newspaper. It was horrible. I still believed my dad at that time, so as well as being scared, I was really angry when people banged on the door of his van or rocked it from side to side when we were inside it, shouting abuse and threats about what should be done to paedophiles. That happened several times when we were in town, and I was threatened a few times when I was on my own, too, by people who knew both of us by sight.

After the threats and abuse started, I stopped going into town on my own and became very suspicious of people in general, which, unfortunately, is something that has stuck with me ever since.

On one occasion, when Fran and I had been out for a meal at lunchtime and were on our way back to her house, I was confronted by the cousin of the drunk who lived in the flat downstairs from the one Dad and I lived in. It must have been about five o'clock in the afternoon and was just getting dark when we passed the bus station, where he was sitting with all the other drunks who used to hang out there. I didn't notice him until he grabbed hold of me and started shouting at me, accusing *me* of being a paedophile too. He was going nuts, and I can remember saying something like, 'Mate, I'm 16 years old. What are you on about?' It was horrible.

Fortunately, another drunk came over and pulled him off, then said, 'Are you all right, boy? It's not you, it's your dad.' I suppose he was trying to be nice, although at the time I hated them both.

The flat I lived in with my dad was on the first floor and had its own front door on the street, which the man who accosted me at the bus station that day would often bang on when he was visiting his cousin downstairs. Then, when he'd got our attention, he would stand on the pavement, shouting abuse and threats up at our windows. It made life very miserable and we'd often sit in the flat with all the lights off, pretending we weren't there.

Whenever we did come and go, we were always very careful to lock the front door and would walk quickly to and from the van, hoping to get into it or the house before anyone saw us. The trouble is, once one person in the street knows something like that, it isn't long before everyone knows about it. Other people didn't really *do* anything, though. It was mainly just the guy who lived in the flat below, his cousin and his girlfriend, although it was only the cousin that shouted at *me*; the other two reserved their verbal abuse for my dad.

There was another really scary occasion when Dad and I were in town, parked near some public toilets, and a group of people saw us and tried to open the doors of the van. Fortunately, we managed to pull them shut and he drove off, with these guys banging on the roof and shouting abuse at us.

It was a lot to deal with at 16, especially when I believed that the foul things people were shouting at me and my dad were unfounded. I still believed what he'd told me. So I was really angry with the people who yelled 'paedophile' at him. I suppose it's human nature – for some people – to want to feel that they've got power over someone else, and what they're really shouting in a situation like that is, 'You're worse than me.'

My girlfriend was brilliant, really supportive through it all. I was very lucky – I couldn't have asked for anyone better at the time. She was of the opinion that there's no smoke without fire and that Heidi wouldn't have made the whole thing up, but she was sensible and sensitive and didn't ever try to push her views on me. 'He's your dad,' she would say whenever we talked about it. 'You know him best.' And, at that point, I really thought I did.

My dad's attitude was more direct, however, and he'd demand to know, 'Do you believe me or do you believe Heidi?' And I'd always tell him the same thing: 'I don't know what to believe. I don't believe you did it. But I don't *know* that you didn't, so I can't give you an answer.'

I must have spoken to Heidi during that period, when I went to my mum's house, but if I did, we didn't talk about what had happened. Then Mum got cancer, and Dad disappeared. The two things weren't connected, of course. By the time Mum picked me up in her car one day and told me about the cancer, he was already talking about leaving.

'It doesn't look as though things are going to work out,' he told me one day. 'If this sticks, I'm going away for years. I'm not going to hang around and let that happen.' He must have been on bail pending trial at that time, after he'd been arrested, and I suppose what he said made sense. Even if he hadn't done what Heidi said he'd done, there wasn't any guarantee that he wouldn't be found guilty and be sent to prison. I was still undecided about who to believe, but I felt sorry for him. Although he didn't let anyone see it, I knew he was running out of energy and feeling very low.

Eventually, he came up with a plan, albeit one that wasn't very carefully thought out – that wasn't really the way he did things. He just told me one day that he was going to load all his equipment into his van, like he normally did when he was playing at a pub somewhere, then drive to the coast to catch a ferry to France. 'Then I might go on down to Spain,' he said, as if he was talking about a holiday rather than absconding while on bail awaiting trial for sexually abusing his daughters.

I was relieved when he told me he was leaving. I don't know whether it was selfish to think that way, but having moved with him when he and Mum divorced, I felt I had to stick by him when it all blew up, and that if he went away, all the other stuff would too. Even so, I was sad that he was going, although I didn't tell him that – it wasn't the sort of thing we would ever have said to each other, or to anyone else for that matter.

He made me swear not to tell anyone what he was going to do, not even my girlfriend, and certainly not Mum. In fact,

I didn't tell Mum the details of what I knew for the next two years. I told my family that I woke up one morning and he'd gone, whereas, in fact, I went to the ferry port with him.

We drove down to the port the day before he was planning to catch the ferry to France, and stayed the night with a friend of his called Bill. Bill's sister had been molested by their dad, so it was perhaps surprising that Bill believed Dad when he told him what he'd been charged with and said Heidi was lying because she hated him.

Bill and a couple of his friends came out drinking with us that evening, and we all got very drunk. Then, the next morning, Dad and I drove to the ferry terminal, where he dropped me off. I tell my children all the time how great they are and how much I love them, but Dad and I didn't ever say things like that to each other, or hug each other, so we just said goodbye. Then I got out of the car and walked across the car park to the toilets, where I shut myself in a cubicle and cried, because he was leaving and because it felt as though I was losing my dad.

Just as I was coming out of the toilet block, I saw him driving across the car park in the opposite direction, away from where the ferries were. So I ran after him and managed to flag him down.

'I couldn't get a ticket,' he told me. 'I didn't think I'd need to book.' It seemed to me to be something most people *would* have done if they needed to leave the country in a hurry. Maybe he was afraid that the police might find out if he booked a ticket in advance, although they hadn't taken his passport, so he obviously wasn't considered to be a flight risk.

He did have a ticket now, though, and while we were waiting for the afternoon ferry, we went into town and had something to eat. Then he dropped me at the train station, and I caught a train home on my own.

Before he left, he gave me his bank card, so that I could transfer money from my account into his whenever he needed it. The plan was that I would take over his business, setting up speaker systems at car shows, country fairs and, occasionally, music venues. I couldn't do it on the same scale as he'd done it, because he'd taken a lot of his equipment with him when he left the country. Fortunately, although I'd promised not to tell anyone he'd gone, he had confided in a couple of his mates, who helped me to run things in his absence. Even with their help, however, I wasn't mature enough at 17 to look after any kind of business and manage money. In fact, I did what my dad had always done and spent everything I earned as soon as I got it, so that I ended up living from week to week.

Dad phoned me maybe three or four times in the few weeks after he left, to tell me that he needed money. And each time he phoned, I transferred about £300 into his bank account.

It was October when he went to France, and for the next three months, I kept my promise to him and didn't tell anyone he'd gone. Then, in the January – at around the same time as the business was starting to fizzle out – I had a phone call from the police, telling me to go down to the police station.

When I got there, they said they knew I'd been sending him money and that if I didn't want to go to prison myself, I'd better stop. I don't know how they knew. Maybe he was supposed to report in at intervals while on bail, which obviously he'd stopped doing. I thought they said they'd had access to my bank account. But when I thought about it recently, I realised it would make more sense if they'd looked at *his* account and seen that I'd transferred money into it.

Although on one level I didn't really care about any of it, I was also a bit scared, which I think was what the police had hoped to achieve when they told me I could be charged as an accessory. So, the next time my dad rang, I told him what had happened and that I wouldn't be able to send him any more money, and he just said, 'Okay.'

'I've got a job,' he told me. But when I asked where he was, he said cryptically, 'Overlooking somewhere nice.' If it *was* a clue, I didn't get it – unless he meant he was in Nice, which I don't think he was.

That was the last time I ever spoke to him.

It wasn't until after I'd been called into the police station and they told me they knew I'd been sending money to my dad that I finally told Mum he'd gone. I'd been worrying a bit about the bills that were mounting up. I hadn't made any attempt to pay them, because they were all in his name, but I felt better about it when Mum said, 'He's decided to do this. It's his choice. All you need to worry about is fending for yourself.'

Not long after I'd had that conversation with Mum, I got home to the flat one day to find that someone had smashed up the front door. The people who used to live downstairs – the ones who gave us all the trouble when my dad was still there – had moved out not long after he'd left, and a very nice family had moved in. And it was my new neighbour who told me that the two guys who had tried to break in had baseball bats and that he'd chased them away.

I held it together while I was talking to my neighbour, but as soon as I got upstairs I broke down. I don't know if a couple of thieves had just happened to choose our flat, or if they hadn't been thieves at all but a couple of men who decided to express their opinion about the paedophile they thought still lived there. Either way, I didn't want to hang around to find out.

All I wanted to do was walk away from it all, like Dad had done, and then I realised there was nothing to stop me from doing just that. So I rang Mum and told her what had happened, and she sent round a friend of hers in a van to help me load up the stuff I wanted to take with me, and then drive me home to my family.

Chloe's like me in that we've never been the sort of people who want to talk about emotions. In fact, the conversation she and I had on the phone after Heidi asked us to tell our side of the story for this book was the longest we'd ever had about what had happened. But my relationship with both my sisters improved after I moved back home, and when Heidi and I did start to talk a bit, it wasn't long before I began to change my perception and realise that Dad had been lying.

Perhaps I'd matured a bit during the couple of years I'd spent in that horrible flat with him, which was why I was able to think about it more rationally and to see it for what it was. Whatever the reason, when I started going over old scenarios in my head, I began to think, 'That isn't right.' From the day he first got arrested, I'd often thought, 'Why would Heidi lie about something like that? And why would the police charge him if they didn't have any proof?' But I didn't really examine all the facts until after he'd gone, even though I knew what Heidi had read in Chloe's diary confirmed a lot of what she'd said herself, about the things he'd done to *her*.

I think the reason I hadn't listened before when Heidi tried to talk to me about it was because I didn't want to know. But the reality was that I couldn't sit on the fence forever.

Chapter Ten

Chloe

It must have been after he was arrested that I saw him in the village one day. I was walking to the shop with a friend when he drove past in the van, then stopped and waited for us to catch up. Mum had told me that he wasn't allowed to speak to me, but he wound down the window and said, 'Oh, you've got a new dog. Where's Lexi?' Tom was sitting next to him, in the passenger seat, but he looked away and didn't say anything. And I didn't either. I just carried on walking, and after hesitating for a moment, my friend scuttled after me.

She didn't know that he'd been arrested or that he was out on bail, so she was completely bemused when she asked me, 'Isn't that your dad? Why didn't you speak to him?' But I just shrugged and kept on walking.

It can't have been very long after that when Mum and Heidi told me I had to see a counsellor, which made me even angrier with Heidi. I told Mum I didn't want to do it, and she said, 'Just go to the first one and see what it's like.'

I spent the whole day before my first session dreading it, and by the time Mum met me off the bus after school I was in tears. She must have taken a break at work, and we sat in the park behind the cathedral while I cried, ate the prawn sandwich she'd bought for me and told her repeatedly that I didn't want to go. I can't remember how she persuaded me, but I do remember crossing the road from the park on my own, then sitting in a cold, dimly lit room until a woman came in and took me to another, equally gloomy room, where I sat in stony silence, deflecting all her attempts to engage me in conversation.

'I could just run out of here,' I thought. 'They wouldn't be able to stop me. I could run away for good.' Then I thought about all the trouble I'd get into and, even more importantly, 'What if he hurt Mum? Or caught *me*?' So I stayed. And as if just being there wasn't bad enough, the woman tried to get me to draw a family tree. I thought she was crazy to believe it could possibly help in any way. It was like saying to me, 'Your father abused you, your sister betrayed your trust, we've all read your secret diary, but never mind, just write the names of your grandparents on this piece of paper and none of it will matter anymore.' Sitting there in that room, I felt as though I was a small child again, screaming to get out, but no one was listening.

Despite the fact that my dread had proved well-founded, I did go back the following week, and this time the woman got me to make some papier mâché balloons and paint my emotions on them. I think the counsellor called it something like 'modelling about my emotions'. To me, though, it was the sort of thing you'd do at preschool, and I can't explain how it made me feel. Even in normal circumstances, no 11-year-old child wants to be treated like a baby. And that's what it felt as though everyone was doing – making me into a baby who had no control over anything.

I hated those sessions more than I can describe. I cried and begged Mum not to make me go to them. I realise now that she was just doing her best for me – or maybe what social services thought was best. And although I might have been wrong, sitting in that room in that dismal building at the end of a dark alleyway doing what seemed to be totally pointless exercises didn't make me feel better about *anything*. In fact, it simply made me feel awkward and uncomfortable.

What I was also very anxious about was the possibility that someone I knew – a friend from school, for example – might see me going into or coming out of the building. None of my friends knew anything about what was happening, and I dreaded the thought of any of them finding out. So I started skiving off school.

Mum left for work at 7.30 most mornings and didn't get home until 6 in the evening. She had no idea that I often stayed at home or got off the bus at the stop before the one for school, then walked to a friend's house where I'd hang out for a couple of hours before going on to school with her.

Then one day I came home in the afternoon to find the hallway almost blocked by a huge mattress, and when I asked Mum what was happening, she told me, 'Tom's moving into the back room. Your dad's gone.'

'Why isn't Tom going back into his bedroom?' I asked her. But I can't remember what she said. Maybe there wasn't

enough room in it for the huge mattress and all the amplifi-
ers and stuff he had with him, which almost filled the room
next to the kitchen, where he never opened the curtains so
that it soon smelled dank and unaired. I used to like going
in there though, despite the vague odour. Things hadn't
ever been awkward between me and Tom and soon after
he came home, it started *feeling* like home again. We never
talked about *him* or what had happened though, and I don't
think we ever have.

As far as *him* skipping bail and leaving the country was
concerned, I think I was a bit torn between being pleased
that I wouldn't have to give evidence in court after all, and
feeling that all the embarrassing stuff that had happened
since Heidi read my diary had been a total waste of time.
But at least it was over and he had gone.

Chapter Eleven

Heidi

After my dad got Tom and one of his own friends to say I'd tried to poison him by putting chemicals in his coffee, Dan, the policeman who was in charge of the case, came to see me.

'No, I didn't try to poison him,' I told Dan.

'I didn't think you had,' he said. 'Don't worry, we're not giving it any credibility. But I had to ask, just for the record.'

What I didn't tell Dan was how many times I'd spat in my dad's coffee, or watched with malicious satisfaction while he ate food I'd pushed around the kitchen floor. But they weren't criminal offences, I reasoned, whereas trying to poison him obviously would have been. And despite how much I hated him, there was only one occasion when I really thought I could have hurt him, even killed him, and not regretted it.

It was after I'd read Chloe's diary, but before I told Mum about it. I'd had a problem with the alternator on my car and I was holding a broken piece of it in my hand when he turned up at the house to take Chloe out somewhere. It was the first time I'd seen him since discovering that he'd abused my little sister, and I suddenly had an overwhelming desire to hit him over the head with the bit of metal I was clutching, and to keep on hitting him until he was dead. I can remember having to squeeze it very tightly in my hand to stop myself doing just that, and it was only after he'd gone that I saw the imprint it had made on my palm and became aware of the painful throbbing in my fingers.

The fact that he'd told the police I'd tried to poison him wasn't surprising or particularly distressing in any way. What did hurt, though, was the thought that Tom believed it. I felt more alone at that time, and more in need of a hug from my mum, than I had ever done before. Chloe hated me, Tom hated me and wouldn't speak to me, my dad hated me – although that was different, because I hated him too – and I didn't seem to have any sort of relationship with Mum at all, even after she knew what he'd done to me.

During what was almost a year since my dad had been arrested and charged, I'd lived in fear of walking around a corner on a street in town one day and coming face to face with him. Chloe had refused to say anything about what he'd done to her. Which meant that if I disappeared or met with an unfortunate accident, the case against him, such as it was, would simply evaporate. It sounds melodramatic to say it now, but it was a real concern for me at the time, and just the thought that it *could* happen made me very jumpy and nervous.

Before I left college, I'd met a guy called Evan, who worked for a boat builder and was heavily into drugs, although I didn't realise then the extent of his many addictions. Smoking weed with Evan, which I did a handful of times, didn't make me feel better about the horrible things that were happening in my life and that I thought I'd caused to happen in other people's lives too, but it did allow me to forget about them – for a while at least. I knew it wasn't the way forward, though, and that the solution to my problems – if, indeed, there was one – certainly wasn't to be found by looking at the world through a haze of cannabis smoke.

When I finished my course and left college, I got four jobs – two at shops in town, one at the local pub and another doing cleaning. Then, the following January, we found out that Dad had left the country, and shortly after that, someone tried to break into his flat and Tom came back to live at home. I assumed Dad had only just upped and left, but as Tom and I ignored each other, I didn't actually ask him what had happened, and he didn't tell me. The reason I didn't speak to him was because I was still very angry, and he made it very clear that he didn't want to speak to me either, so it was weird having him at home again.

After Tom moved back in, I snooped again and read his mail. What I discovered this time – from the mobile phone bills that were being redirected to him – was that Dad was either in France or Spain. And when I looked at Tom's bank statement, I saw that he'd been transferring money into Dad's account. So I reported my dad to social security, because I knew he was still getting unemployment benefits. Then I told Dan what I'd discovered.

I was quite friendly with Tom's girlfriend, Fran, and when I saw her a few days later and told her what I'd done, she was frosty with me. I don't think I understood at the time that it was the snooping she objected to. I suppose it's a bit like having OCD: you might know on an intellectual

level that you don't need to keep washing your hands or
checking you've locked the door or turned off the kettle,
but what would happen if one day you didn't check and you
hadn't done one of those things? The compulsion was similar for me, in that I thought I had to know everything about
everything that was happening so that I didn't miss something important. It had started when I was a child, when it
felt as if things were spinning out of control, and it got worse
when I discovered that Chloe had been abused by her dad.

Tom didn't see it that way, of course, and when he rang
me from Fran's that evening, he was really nasty to me. It
must have been after his call that I wrote in my diary:

> How can I treat him with the love and respect I want
> to when he's protecting the enemy? … Mum is still
> being a bit funny with me. In some ways she tries,
> but in other ways I feel I'm being blamed for Chloe,
> which makes me feel bad, because I don't blame *her*
> [Mum]. She seems to show Chloe a lot of love and
> affection, even when Chloe's rude and nasty. You
> can tell she isn't even slightly interested, but she still
> gets all the cuddles. I think if my mum did show me
> even a small amount of affection though, I wouldn't
> be able to cope with it, because I'm not used to it.
> In fact, even now, I find I'm too timid to show my
> feelings at all.

It seemed that, for years, I'd been telling myself, 'One day,
something will happen to make it all change.' But it never

did. The harder I tried, the worse everything became, until eventually I had no one.

By the time Tom came home, I'd got a job writing about places of interest for the website of a local travel company. I was in one of their offices in another town one day when I received a message saying that my mum wanted me to phone her. I thought it might have something to do with my dad, so I went into the toilets to make the call.

'I've just been to the hospital,' Mum told me. 'I've got a lump in my breast and they think it could be cancer.'

I stayed in that toilet for several minutes afterwards, crying. What I wanted to do was go straight home to be with my mum, but someone had driven me to the office, which was some distance from where we lived, and we were due to stay at a colleague's house that night, so I didn't see Mum until the next day. I'd already begun researching, and I continued for the next few weeks in a determined quest to find some nugget of information somewhere that would enable me to fix her, or at least to reduce the effects of the treatment she subsequently had.

Within days, the lump had been removed and Mum was facing further treatment with radiotherapy and chemotherapy. I was convinced that the cancer had been caused by all the stress she'd been subjected to, and I really wanted to be there for her during that time. It was what I was always trying to do anyway – not say or do anything that might hurt her feelings, not go out at night so that she wasn't left on her own. I just wanted to protect her and make everything better for her. And I was determined not to give up, however little affection she showed me in return. It was difficult sometimes, though, when I was trying really hard and she kept pushing me away.

Then, one day, Mum had just had a chemotherapy session and was upstairs in bed, feeling quite ill, and I was lying on the floor in the lounge with my legs up on the couch, when Tom came into the room and lay down beside me, in exactly the same position.

He didn't say anything, but the silence between us felt different somehow, and after a couple of minutes I broke it by saying, 'I'm finding this very difficult. We haven't spoken for such a long time. But now that we're living in the same house, it would be really nice to talk.' So that's what we did, for the first time in months. We talked about mostly general things that day, and a bit about Mum, and we made a plan to sort out the garden for her.

Mum had a bad time with the chemotherapy and I'd been doing a lot of research into how to reduce or deal with its effects. But doing the garden was something practical we could do for her, and something the three of us could do together, as Chloe helped too. We spent an entire day clearing it, then trying to make it nice so that Mum could sit in it when she was better. I think that day was a significant turning point for all of us, working as a unit after so many months of not even speaking to each other.

People say that, sometimes, good things can come from bad beginnings, and although Mum's cancer experience was horrible, I don't know whether Tom, Chloe and I would ever have reconnected again if *something* hadn't happened at that time to bring us together the way it did. After we'd done the garden, we really made an effort to keep talking to each other, not about anything deep and meaningful, but because talking about *anything* involved spending time together and starting to rebuild our relationship.

Mum's cancer treatment continued for several months, and it was just coming to an end when I went to university. I had been accepted by the university that had been my first choice when I applied, but it was a four-hour drive from home and I didn't want to be that far away after Mum had been so ill. So I went to one that was just over an hour's drive away, which meant that I was far enough from home not to have to live every day with the feeling I often had of being useful in a crisis but otherwise not really loved by my family, and yet close enough to be able to step in and save the day if the need arose for the services of the superhero I think I always wanted to be!

There were lots of things I enjoyed about my time at university, including making some amazing friends while I was there. But as well as studying for my degree in marketing, I was doing four jobs, all of which I enjoyed, but which meant I was working very hard. The first job, which I started almost as soon as I got to university, involved working for a media company three evenings a week, from 5 to 11 p.m. Then I got another, working two evenings a week in the university bar; then another, doing marketing for a big company; and a fourth, working for a charity, doing craft workshops with children and being a student ambassador as part of a scheme to raise their expectations in life and make them realise they could do anything they set their minds to doing. I continued to do all four jobs throughout my time at university. The only downside was that I had to stay there for the holidays when everyone else went home, which was quite lonely. But at least it meant I didn't ever have to worry about how I was going to pay my rent and other living expenses. In term time, I had a good social life too.

Being so close to home, I had a constant feeling that I might turn around one day and find Dad standing behind me. Although it was good to know that I could get home and be there for my family at the drop of a hat, I was also always alert to the fact that he might be out there some-where, watching me. I asked Tom a couple of times if he knew where he was, but he said he didn't, and I spent the next three years looking over my shoulder. In fact, there were several occasions when I thought I saw him. It wasn't him, of course, but for a few seconds each time I felt sick and overwhelmed by a sense of panic.

Apart from that, I began to feel quite liberated while I was away at university, almost as though I'd es-caped. It must have been good for my self-confidence too, because for the first time in my life I broke off a relationship – with Evan – rather than being the one who was dumped. Then, after going out with someone else on a not very serious basis for a while, I met Liam, who I idolised from a distance for a couple of months before we started going out. With Liam, I felt my life was moving forward at last, and that I really might be able to leave the past behind me after all.

Another significant relationship I had at that time was with a girl called Zoe, who lived in the same hall of residence as I did. I didn't tell people about my father – I wanted their judgements about me to be based on *me*, not on something that had happened *to* me when I was a child. I did tell Liam everything, though. And Zoe, who had been abused by *her* dad, and who quickly became a very close friend.

While we were still at university, Zoe's father became very ill and she decided she had to go home. Apparently, he was in a bad way when she got there and couldn't speak, and when he died a few days later, she went to his funeral. I think I felt angry with her when she told me she was going home; I certainly couldn't understand why she wanted to see him. And I thought she'd be glad when he died – I knew *I* would be if my father died – but she was really upset and said she'd done the right thing, which didn't seem to make any sense to me.

Then, one day, when I was at home during a university holiday, working for a temp agency in town, Mum rang me and said Dad had phoned his friend Keith, who had then rung Mum to tell her Dad was dying of cancer. As she was talking to me on the phone, I suddenly felt sick, and incredibly upset. But when we didn't hear anything more about it, I began to suspect that it had all been a lie. Maybe he had hoped to elicit sympathy, or maybe he wanted to make us feel bad about the fact that he was trapped somewhere abroad and on his own, if that *was* still the case.

***

After I finished university, Liam had another year to go, so I went home – not to Mum's house, but to share a rented cottage in the same village with a friend. I couldn't find a job I really wanted to do – something that involved project management for a media company or writing for a magazine or website. So I worked for a while at a credit company, phoning people up and saying, 'Hello, there. Do you have debts?' Then, if the answer was, 'Yes, I've got one credit card and 12 store cards' – as was surprisingly often the case – I would tell them, 'Well, that's great. Let's put all those debts into just one loan for you.'

It was mind-numbing, soul-destroying work, and the first time I'd done anything I hadn't enjoyed and taken pride in. What I hated most about it was that I felt as though I was ripping people off, trying to make it sound as though it would be a good thing for them to consolidate all their debts, despite the fact that by doing so they would probably increase both their interest rate and the term of their repayments. And as well as making me feel guilty, it was tedious, repetitive work, reading the same script off a computer screen over and over again to people who seemed to have been selected specifically because they were unlikely to ask the questions they should have asked. I got some pretty horrible verbal abuse too, and some heavy breathing down the phone.

After feeling so optimistic while I was at university, and beginning to look forward to a bright, self-determined future, I now found myself in the position of having a degree but doing a job I hated, with no apparent prospect of getting a better one.

After about a year of alternating between fielding the – perfectly justified – verbal onslaughts of people who were busy doing something else when I phoned them, and consolidating the debts of the very indebted, I got two good job offers on the same day. I took the one that involved both writing and project management, and moved to a town a couple of hours' drive away from home.

During that year, I'd been travelling backwards and forwards to spend time with Liam, who finished university just before I got the good job, so we were able to move together. Suddenly, it felt as though the future was back on track.

There was one incident that occurred during those months when I was living in the village again that has always stuck in my mind. Mum, Tom, Chloe, Nanny, Granddad and I had had lunch at a hotel in a seaside town and were walking back along the beach, looking at all the sandcastles people were building as part of a competition, when Nanny turned to me and started to say something, then stopped.

'What?' I asked, taking her arm. 'What were you going to say, Nan?'

'Oh, nothing,' she said, blushing slightly and turning her head away.

'It's okay.' I hugged her arm closer to mine for a moment. 'You can tell me, whatever it is.'

'Well …' She hesitated, then seemed to make a decision and said, 'I was just going to say that your dad always loved building sandcastles with you. He used to spend hours doing it.'

'That's good to know,' I told her. 'I think everyone has *some* good in them. So I'm glad you told me that. Thank you.'

Not long after that day – and a couple of years after he'd rung his friend and said he had cancer – my dad phoned Mum and said he needed to speak to Tom or to his own brother, George, urgently. I don't think it was a long conversation, and I don't think he did talk to either Tom or George. Then, a couple of weeks later, my counsellor Lesley rang and told me he'd walked up to a policeman in a city about 15 miles from home and said, 'I believe I'm wanted.'

Chapter Twelve

Heidi

I think he was homeless and living on the streets when he handed himself in. According to the policeman who arrested him, he looked like a tramp. He certainly looked very different from the way I remembered him in the photograph that was taken of him at the police station. Something had obviously happened during the five years he'd been away.

Chloe was 16 when he came back. And this time when I told her, 'He won't be put away if you don't talk, because it will just be my word against his,' I felt incredibly proud of her when she agreed to give a statement.

The case went to court almost six months after I'd received the phone call from Lesley. I hadn't realised how badly the whole thing would affect me, and I often found myself stuttering and stumbling over words when I tried to speak, as if they were lost in a vacuum somewhere between my brain and my mouth. In fact, I became so stressed and nervous that I was put on beta blockers, to stop my heart racing and the blood pounding in my ears.

There was no real support during that time – except from Lesley, who was still my counsellor and friend – and no one told me what to expect when I went to court. All I knew about it was what I'd seen on TV programmes, which often show witnesses being challenged aggressively by defendants' lawyers.

After I read Chloe's diary and he was arrested for the first time, I said in a witness statement: 'I have been told that there is a possibility that I might be protected from being seen by my abuser while giving evidence in the court. I feel I would be intimidated and scared if I were able to be seen by him while giving my evidence. I am determined that I will attend the court to give my evidence, but it would make the whole experience less frightening if I were able to be screened from him.'

By the time the case finally went to court, six years later, I had changed my mind. Despite the stress of it all, I was still determined to give my evidence in the courtroom, but now I wanted him to be able to see me, so that he would know I wasn't frightened of him or intimidated by him anymore. I had spent the last few years dreading what was about to happen, but, at the same time, I had been waiting for it.

I spent the night before the first day of the trial at Lesley's house and she went with me to the court the next morning. In fact, she sat in the courtroom every day throughout the hearing and was the only one of us to do so, as Mum didn't go in at all, and Chloe and I weren't allowed to listen to each other giving our evidence.

When Lesley and I arrived at the court on the first day, Mum and Chloe were already there. But Tom wasn't. 'Where is he?' I asked Mum, anxiously. 'He *is* coming, isn't he? I thought he'd come.' During the last five years, since we'd started talking to each other again, Tom and I had become really close, particularly when I was at university and every time he visited me we'd gone out and got drunk together, and talked even more.

I knew it must have been incredibly difficult for him to accept the truth about his dad, so I'd had very mixed feelings – which included sympathy and relief – when I realised that he did believe me, and Chloe too. When he didn't turn up at the court that first morning, the already huge ordeal I was facing suddenly seemed insurmountable.

It takes a lot to upset me so much that my distress becomes visible to other people. Perhaps Mum saw it, though, because I think she phoned Tom. If she did, whatever she said to him must have struck a chord, because we were still sitting on the wooden chairs outside the courtroom when he turned up. And as soon as he was there, everything seemed possible again. Or, at least, not as *im*possible as it had started to feel before he came.

Liam had asked if I wanted him to go with me to the hearing, but I had pulled my superhero cape more tightly around me and said, 'No.' It's the sort of thing I often do on occasions when I really need some support. Then Liam had also said what he almost always said, which was, 'Okay, Heidi. I'm fine with whatever you want to do.'

Chloe and I had to stay apart, as we weren't allowed to talk to each other before we gave our evidence, so she had lunch with Mum, while Lesley took Tom and me to a nice restaurant just down the road from the courthouse. It was the first time Tom and Lesley had met, and I can remember looking at them both while we were sitting in the restaurant that day and getting a really strong sense that we were united. Chloe had Mum's support, as she had always done, and now I had Tom to support me – and Lesley too, of course. There was no avoiding the fact that the next few days were going to be an ordeal, but it was an ordeal I felt a bit more prepared to face now that I knew my brother was on my side.

The court hearing lasted for three days. Chloe gave her evidence on the first day, Dad gave his on the second, and I gave mine on the third. I wasn't in the courtroom when he was giving his evidence. I can't remember now if that was because I wasn't allowed to go in, or because I didn't want to. Lesley was there, though, and I know she was disgusted by the things he said and by his absolute refusal to take any responsibility for what he'd done.

'He's in complete denial,' she told me afterwards. 'At one point, he answered a question by looking at the palms of his hands and saying, dramatically, "These hands never touched my children." Then he held them out to the jury and said, "These hands? I cannot imagine them doing the things that have been described."' Later, apparently, after saying how much he loved his family, he was asked when his children were born and he had no idea. 'His attitude throughout was almost dismissive, and I don't think he ever showed any kind of emotion at all,' Lesley told me.

I can't remember very much about my part of it, except that as soon as I walked into the courtroom, I felt as though

I was seven years old again. For example, I would normally refer to a penis as a penis, without any hesitation or embarrassment. But my vocabulary seemed to have shrunk and I had lost the ability to talk like an adult, so I couldn't think what to call it at all.

What I do remember is how proud I felt of Chloe and Tom when his barrister asked me about them, and how determined I was to make sure he knew I'd gone to university and got a degree. My dad had told me many times that I would never go to university or 'amount to much' in any other way. So I wanted to prove to him that he'd been wrong and that although I might have been damaged by what he'd done to me, I hadn't, by any means, been destroyed by it.

I'd waited a long time to give my evidence and I made sure I looked directly at him while I did it. It was a surreal experience though, particularly when his barrister asked me questions that were obviously carefully worded to make me seem like an attention-seeking hysteric who had made the whole thing up. What helped a bit, however, was the fact that I could see the jury, because I could tell from their faces that they believed me, especially one woman, who sometimes put her head in her hands, then looked at him across the courtroom with an expression of appalled disgust.

It didn't take the jury very long to find him guilty – on 13 counts. But, for me, the worst part was still to come.

I hadn't realised that, when Tom finally came into the courtroom to hear his dad being sentenced, they would read out each of the counts of which he'd been found guilty. It was horrible to have to sit there knowing that my brother was hearing for the first time details of what his father had done to his sisters. What also surprised me was that I'd expected to feel relieved, knowing that I'd be able to put it all behind me at last, whereas what I actually felt was incredibly sad. I'd kept his secret for all those years because I thought I was protecting my family. Now they all knew, and those years had been wasted.

But it was Tom I felt most sorry for, sitting there beside me on the crowded courtroom bench in his black suit, with his legs shaking violently. I had hated my dad for many years, but Tom had loved him. How must he feel now, I wondered, listening to the terrible proof of what sort of man his father really was?

'If only you'd just done it to me and left Chloe alone,' I thought, as I looked across the courtroom through my tears at the dishevelled, emotionless figure of my father, 'Tom wouldn't have had to deal with any of this and he'd still be happy.'

Before the judge passed sentence on each of the 13 counts of indecent assault or offence of indecency with children, he gave his 'observations'. Our ages when the assaults occurred – between 7 and 13 for me, and 7 and 10 for Chloe – were a significant factor, the judge told him, as was the gross breach of trust by a father, whose obligations in life include protecting his children, whereas he had used his children's love for him in order to abuse them.

The defendant's own barrister had acknowledged the fact that his client had stolen his daughters' innocence as well as their happiness, the judge said. Then he described some of the things our father had done to us, which were difficult enough for me to sit and listen to, but which must have been horrific for Tom to have to hear.

The most serious offence, the judge continued, was requiring me to perform oral sex on him and then ejaculating into my mouth. Under the terms of legislation that had come into effect quite recently, that offence would be charged as rape, the judge said, which would, on its own, have justified a sentence of seven years. But all the offences had to be charged under the old legislation that was in force when he committed them, although, even so, they were serious enough to warrant imprisonment.

For each of the charges that related to me, he was sentenced to three years, plus five years for the more serious count that amounted to rape – all of which were to run concurrently. On each of the three charges in relation to Chloe, he was given a sentence of two years – again, all concurrent to each other. So, basically, five years for all the years he'd been abusing me, and two years for what he'd done to Chloe. Which made a grand total of seven years in prison – of which, Lesley explained to me afterwards, he would probably only serve three and a half. It was some small consolation to know that when he was released, he would be banned from working with children and would have to report to a police station every 12 months for the rest of his life.

I've never really understood how lawyers are able to cross-examine witnesses the way they do, or how they can speak so eloquently in defence of clients they must sometimes strongly suspect are guilty of the appalling crimes they've been accused of. But even though I know that's the job they're paid to do, I was still surprised when someone told me that, as my father's barrister was leaving the courtroom, he apparently referred to his client as 'a little shit' who had got what he deserved, and said he was glad he'd gone down.

When we walked out of the courtroom, I felt strangely disorientated to find that the sun was shining. The fact that the world was still revolving and life was going on as normal seemed wrong somehow. Then, as we walked towards the steps, I saw a man and a woman who I recognised as having been members of the jury. They were standing in the sunshine smoking cigarettes, and as we passed them, the woman said to me, 'You go on and have a good life now, love.' And although I wanted to say something to *her*, to let her know that I appreciated her concern, I found I couldn't speak.

I'd waited many years to see justice being served and I always thought I'd have a deep sense of satisfaction if it ever was. But the damage had already been done – to all of us – and although I'd believed that if this moment did come, everything would change, the reality was that nothing had.

People told me afterwards, 'He'll find out what it's like to be on the receiving end when he gets beaten up in prison.' I knew they were just trying to be nice and to show that they were on my side. But although I'd hated him for years with an anger that had gone off the scale when I found out what he'd been doing to Chloe, those feelings suddenly seemed to have evaporated and I was left with a deep sense of sadness and regret for something I couldn't really understand or explain, as if I'd lost something that had never really existed.

Chapter Thirteen

Chloe

He phoned the house one day when he was on the run. When I first tried to remember what happened, I thought I had answered the phone, but I don't think I did – I think it's one of those memories that has become confused, in the way they sometimes do when you can hear the words in your head and aren't certain whether *you* said them or someone else told you *they* had said them. What I do remember is Mum telling me, 'He said he's got "the big C" and he's dying.'

Mum had cancer herself by that time, so it was all a bit weird. I did wonder if perhaps he knew she was ill, and he was just saying he was, too, in some twisted attempt to get sympathy. But, whatever the truth of it was, he handed himself in a few weeks later.

So then the court case was on again, and someone came to the house to take my statement. I don't think I said very much, and although I remember that Mum was there and we all sat in the lounge, I don't actually have any memory of *being* there myself at all.

The case went to court just before I did my GCSEs, so I must have been 16. I was surprised when I thought about that recently, because I'd have said I was older than that when it happened. But Heidi will know exactly when it was. I think she came back from university for the trial, or maybe it was after she'd finished her degree and had started working. I know Tom was still living at home with Mum and me, but he wasn't with us when we left the house to go to the court on the first morning.

Then Mum rang him when we got to the courthouse and I can remember very vividly hearing her say, 'Your sisters need you,' and what felt like just a couple of minutes later, he was there, nodding and asking, 'All right?' And suddenly it *did* feel all right. With Tom there, our family was together, and it felt as though a huge weight had been lifted. Tom believed us and had come to show that he supported us, and I didn't need to be frightened anymore.

Tom didn't go into the courtroom until the sentencing. At the time I was too anxious to think about it from anyone's point of view except mine, but it must have been incredibly difficult for him to be there at all, and I really appreciated the fact that he'd come. I haven't ever said anything to him about it, though: we've never talked about the trial. Tom and I are true Hardings in that respect. In fact, we took the name Harding – which is our mum's name – later, when we had families of our own and didn't want our children to have any connection with *him*. And it's a Harding trait, which Mum shares, not talking about anything awkward, emotional or otherwise potentially uncomfortable. It's only Heidi who finds it difficult to look the other way and not comment when there's an elephant in the room. I think she hates not being able to talk things through almost as much as we hate being asked to do so. She's more like Mum's mum in that respect, who is a Harding only by marriage.

Anyway, not long after Tom arrived at the courthouse, I was called to give my evidence. Someone had explained to me what would happen, but I must have misunderstood and I thought I was going to be in the courtroom itself, behind a screen, whereas in fact I was in a completely separate room, with a TV and video link. All I could see was *his* lawyer and the judge. I was so relieved. But even though it was nothing like the nightmare I'd imagined it would be, it *was* still a nightmare, and very embarrassing.

Some of the questions his lawyer asked me were quite aggressive and intrusive. For example, he kept insisting, 'You've made all this up, haven't you?', which made me really angry. In fact, I think I actually said out loud what I was thinking, which was, 'Why would I make it up when it's destroying my family?'

I did make up some of the story at the back of my diary, but I'd already told them that. So then he asked me questions about *why* I'd made up a story like that and why I'd stuck photographs over what I'd written. I didn't have an answer to the first question. I imagine a psychologist might have been able to think of one, though: there must be some reason why an 11-year-old child would write a love story about herself and her dad that ends in them having sex.

Almost everyone in the courtroom seemed to have a copy of that diary, and I can remember sitting in front of the screen, listening to the lawyer reading out everything I'd written in it and feeling as though I wanted to curl up and die of shame and humiliation. I think I ended up shouting at him to shut up, telling him to stop reading it out loud because I knew what I'd written. Or maybe I only said that bit in my head, although I do have a memory of the judge telling me, 'We need to read out the whole script. I'm sorry, I know it's difficult for you.' But he didn't explain *why* it was necessary. And that was the question that kept coming into my mind as I sat there listening to the lawyer apparently trying to make out that what had happened had somehow been *my* fault: 'Why?'

I think everything I'd written on the first of the two pages at the back of the diary was true. Then, on the second page, I'd added to the truth and made it into a story. Although I hated his barrister at the time for insisting that I'd made it all up and that nothing I'd written on either page was true, I can see now why he might have thought that was the case. What I also wonder now is whether the reason I wrote what I did when I was 11 years old was because, as the result of what must have been a rather bizarre thought process, I believed that by making it into a love story, what *he*'d done wouldn't seem so bad.

It felt as though I was sitting in front of the courtroom screen for a long time. Oddly though, when it was over, it didn't seem to have been very long at all. I was crying for most of the time while I was giving my evidence, and I can remember thinking, 'I hope he can't see me.' They told me he couldn't, but in my head I was certain that he could.

I was still crying when I stood up and walked out of the room, despite the fact – or maybe because of it – that it felt as though the massive weight that had been pressing down on me had suddenly been lifted. The relief of knowing that it was all over and I wouldn't ever have to do that again was incredible.

I think I was the only one who gave evidence that day – Heidi had either already given hers or she did it the following day. I know I felt angry with her, because I thought she was lying to me again when she said she hadn't gone into the courtroom while I was being cross-examined. I didn't mind her counsellor, Lesley, being there, but I didn't want Mum or Tom or Heidi to hear what I was saying. And although Heidi swore that she hadn't heard it, I was certain that she had.

On the last day of the hearing, after we knew the jury had found him guilty on several counts, Mum, Heidi, Tom and I all went into the courtroom together to listen to the sentencing. It was the first time I'd seen *him* since he'd come back from wherever he'd been for the last four or five years, and he didn't look at all like I remembered him. But as I didn't want to make eye contact with him, I didn't really *see* him – I just glanced quickly in his direction, then looked away, in case he turned his head to look at *us*.

While we were listening to the sentences being read out and explained by the judge, I kept wondering what Tom was thinking. I felt really sorry for him, because I knew he was losing his dad. In fact, I thought it must be even harder for Tom than it was for Heidi and me, as we'd lost *him* years ago – when Heidi found my diary and he was arrested, in my case – whereas Tom had believed in him for all those years, maybe until that day, when he heard for the first time what his dad had done and had now been found guilty of doing, 'beyond a reasonable doubt'.

It was horrible sitting there during the judge's summing-up, which included things I wouldn't ever have wanted Tom to know about, and that I'm certain he didn't want to hear. Then the judge added up all the separate sentences and when the total came to just seven years, I can remember thinking, 'Why did I bother? Why did I go through all that for what amounts to little more than nothing?' I felt even worse about it later, when someone explained that he would only actually serve half of the sentence. Three-and-a-half years in prison doesn't seem much of a punishment for ruining the childhoods of both his daughters and for robbing them of the chance to have had a real dad.

I know Heidi felt the same way about the short sentence, and after I'd absorbed the initial shock and disappointment, I began to blame myself for it and to think, 'If only I'd given more evidence, he might have got longer.' But I'd told them everything I could remember, so I didn't know what else I could have done. Maybe if I'd had the sort of counselling Heidi had been having, I could have remembered more. But if I *had* had counselling, I might have been faced with the prospect of having to spend the rest of my life trying to deal with all the stuff I'd dragged up from my subconscious into my conscious mind, and he still might only have got a few years.

What hurt more than anything was the fact that I thought only one of the seven years of his sentence was for the things he'd done to me. So, just 6 of the 42 months, at most, that he'd actually spend in prison. What was the point? It felt as though all the humiliation and misery I'd been subjected to – first by *him*, then by having to defend myself against a barrage of aggressive questioning by his apparently disbelieving barrister in a courtroom full of people – had been for nothing.

Even now, 12 years later, I still feel as if I'm being abused by him. Not physically, of course, but because he took away so much of my life and robbed me of so many things I should have had. I don't think anything could ever make up for what I've lost. Because of him, I haven't got a nice father like most of my friends have, and my children won't ever have a grandfather who loves and cares about them. And in exchange for stealing my life, he spent just six months in prison. That's not justice. That's not fair.

Although I can remember walking out of the courtroom that day, I have no memory at all of going home, eating a meal or going to bed. I think I was too exhausted to focus on anything other than the disappointment and hurt.

I didn't talk to anyone about what had happened – not Heidi and not any of my friends. Life just carried on pretty much as normal after that. A few weeks later, I did my GCSEs, left school and got a job in a shop. I was already working part-time in a supermarket, and going out with a horrible boy who said to me one day, 'He didn't get done for what he did to you, did he? It was just for your sister.'

'You're wrong,' I told him. 'It said in the newspaper that it was for both of us.'

But I couldn't shake off the feeling that it wasn't. I was worried, too, because I thought everyone knew about what had happened, even though the report in the newspaper hadn't mentioned any names. People in the village were certainly aware of it – things get round pretty quickly in a small community like the one we lived in. But none of my friends ever mentioned it to me at all. *He* had already gone off to Spain or wherever it was by the time I started secondary school, so none of the new friends I'd made knew him or anything about him. Nor did the people I worked with in the supermarket, who were bemused but sympathetic when I suddenly ran into the toilet so that they wouldn't know I was crying the day I saw the headline about his conviction in the local paper.

I was still working in the same supermarket about four years later when *his* barrister came in – the one I'd felt so resentful towards when he asked me all those nasty questions during the trial. He didn't recognise me, of course; but I knew it was him as soon as I saw him. It was a weird experience, having to pretend not to know who he was and serve him the way I would any other customer. I don't know how I managed to get through it, and as soon as he walked away from my till, I excused myself and, once again, hid in the toilet crying as I waited for all the memories that had been triggered to stop tumbling around inside my head.

I told all the new friends I made after I finished school that I didn't have a dad – I think I said he was dead. So I didn't have to try to explain to anyone why I cried in the supermarket yet again when all the Father's Day cards were put out on display. Mum was already worried about me by that time, and a few days after I told her what had happened, she met me from work, took me out to lunch and said, 'I think you're depressed.' Then she handed me a leaflet and I burst into tears.

Chapter Fourteen

Tom

After my girlfriend Fran and I split up, when I was 18, I spent most of my spare time partying. In fact, that's what I did for the next six or seven years, and when I moved back into Mum's I can remember thinking, 'I will never again work at weekends', which was when most of the work I'd done for Dad had taken place. So I did some gardening jobs during the week, then worked for a while in telesales. For me in those days, work was only ever a means to an end: if I got paid on a Friday, I'd have spent almost all of it by the Sunday. Partying wasn't an escape, though. It wasn't something I did to cover up some kind of emotional distress – I was actually happy and enjoying myself.

I must have done the telesales job for about three months. Then, one Monday, I packed it in and went to the pub, and while I was there I got a call from a friend who was working in Denmark. When I told him I'd just quit my job, he asked if I wanted to work with him, doing boat repairs, and I left England the following Tuesday. I stayed in Denmark for about eight months, which I really enjoyed, and it wasn't until about eight years ago that my life started to have any clear direction.

I hadn't had any contact with my dad at all since his last phone call, when I'd told him I couldn't send him any more money. Then, about five years after he'd left the country, he phoned my mum and said he needed to speak to me or to his friend Keith urgently. My memory of events during that period, when I was drinking a lot, isn't very good, but I think he just spoke to Mum – I know I didn't talk to him. 'He sounded really drunk and disorientated,' she told me afterwards. 'He said he's got cancer and he's dying.'

Mum had had breast cancer by that time, so I wasn't sure what to make of it. And obviously she wasn't either, because I can remember her saying, 'I don't know what to believe. I'll pass on his messages for him, but other than that I wash my hands of it all.'

I think the best word I can think of to describe how I felt after his phone call is conflicted. On the one hand, I wanted to visit him and to care that he was ill. On the other, I didn't want to see him because I knew I wouldn't be able to look him in the face. I spent a lot of time thinking about it, and decided in the end that there had been too many lies and betrayals that couldn't be ignored or overcome, and that it was too late to try to start any kind of dialogue with him. Even if what he told Mum was true and he really was dying, I couldn't get past the anger I still felt for him. Mentally, I'd forgotten about him, and judging from the fact that he hadn't tried to contact me after I stopped sending him money, he had forgotten about me too. It seemed to me that we were already dead to each other.

When Heidi told me he'd handed himself in, I was a bit … not annoyed exactly, I just didn't want it all coming up again. I didn't know whether he actually did have cancer, whether he genuinely thought he did or whether he had simply got to the point where he couldn't go on living wherever he'd been living for the past five years. What I *did* know was that, now that he was back, the case against him would go ahead. Which meant that I was going to be put in a situation I didn't want to be in and would have to face something I didn't want to face.

The reality wasn't nearly as bad that time, though. When I'd been living with him, before he left the country, I felt as though I had to support him, and that I was almost as much of a target of people's accusations as he was. But I was a completely different person once I went back home to live with Mum. A couple of my close mates knew my dad had been arrested and had then fled the country, but most of my other friends didn't know anything about it. During the time he'd been away, I'd felt able to separate myself from it a bit more than had seemed possible in the past, thanks to time and growing up a bit, I suppose.

I was at the courthouse throughout the trial. Not in the courtroom itself – Chloe didn't want me in there when she was giving her evidence, and I could understand why. Your siblings are always present in your life, and it would be embarrassing to have to talk about something in front of them that you didn't really want them to know. You'd be worrying about it every time you saw them afterwards, in case what they'd heard had changed their opinion of you, even if it was about something that wasn't your fault. So I told both my sisters, 'To be honest, I don't want to go in at all until the end.' And then I sat outside.

After he'd been found guilty of several charges, Heidi asked if I was going to go in for the sentencing and I told her, honestly, 'I don't know.'

'I want you to be there,' she said. 'But it's your choice.'

'I do too,' Chloe told me.

I knew that Chloe, particularly, would hate having to talk in front of other people in any circumstances, even about something ordinary and impersonal. Giving their evidence and being cross-examined by his barrister must have been really difficult for them both and I think they did incredibly well to go through with it. So, after what they'd been through, not going into the courtroom with them for the sentencing didn't seem to be an option: it was just something I had to do.

I had approached the question of his guilt the same way I think about any dilemma – by asking myself some logical questions. In this case, the pivotal question was: did my dad do those things to my sisters or were Heidi and Chloe both lying? It was a question I didn't try to answer for a long time, which was the cause of a lot of the arguments I'd had with him before he left the country. In fact, he'd got so frustrated with my refusal to come down on one side or the other that, one day, he had packed all my stuff into a suitcase, thrown it down the stairs in the flat and shouted at me, 'You can't go on sitting on the fence like this. If you don't believe that Heidi's lying, you need to get out.'

'But I *can* sit on the fence,' I'd told him, picking up the suitcase and carrying it back up the stairs. 'There doesn't have to be a yes-or-no answer. I can quite easily be on *both* sides: I can go and see my mum and I can stay with you. I don't have to decide who's telling the truth. In fact, I can sit on the fence for as long as I want to.'

I was taller than he was by that time, and just as strong, so I knew that he couldn't physically throw me out, which I imagine he'd have liked to have done, because he must have hated not knowing what I really believed. He was someone who needed to know that people liked him. So although I think he did like having me there before it all happened, he wanted me out by that point, not least because, having lied to me, he still had to deal with me every day. I didn't question him about it at all, but he must have wondered what I was thinking and whether I knew he really had done the things to his own daughters he so vehemently denied. I'm sure that's something anyone in his position would have wondered about, even someone who wasn't as paranoid by nature as he was.

By the time he came back to England and gave himself up to the police, I'd landed squarely on Heidi and Chloe's side of the fence. I wouldn't have gone into the courtroom to hear the sentencing if I hadn't believed 100 per cent that he was guilty. I was there for only one reason – to support my sisters. Even so, I think that when he was found guilty, it was like the final confirmation. I hadn't ever really doubted what Heidi and Chloe said, but now I *knew* it was true.

Throughout the trial itself, we sat on benches just out-side the courtroom, with our backs against the wall. Chloe was really scared when it came to her turn to go in. And I remember being surprised when Heidi gave me a hug, be-cause hugging is something we didn't ever do. I suppose it was the first time I'd shown that I really was on their side. Then Mum hugged me too.

It had all been too much for me to deal with before then. It had felt as though everything had been building up in layers, or that a web was being spun around me by lies – his and my own. It started when he was first arrested and I told Heidi, 'You've got to stop lying. If you don't, Dad's going to tell the police that you tried to poison him.' I was speaking from the script he'd given me and didn't really believe she'd been putting cleaning chemicals in his coffee. But once you tell a lie, you have to be very careful not to trip yourself up by saying something that contradicts what you've forgotten you've said. I think that's why I tried to avoid talking about it at all after I'd said that to Heidi. Or it's part of the reason, anyway.

I was a bit scared at the prospect of being in the court-room for the sentencing. Until quite recently, I'd loved my dad, and I'd had some good times with him when I was a child. But I hadn't seen him for five years by then, and I'd changed. It was a strange feeling, as though I'd gone from being on his side to being against him with nothing in be-tween. But I think I can be like that sometimes – quite cold – and I was almost able to say, 'I don't love you anymore. I'm here now, in this place in my life. I've gone past the stage of worrying about you. Whatever you've done is your responsibility.'

Heidi and Chloe were both nervous when we went into the courtroom to listen to the sentencing – Chloe even more so than Heidi, I think. We had already sat down when he came in, and as I watched him shuffling towards his chair, I was taken aback by how much he'd aged and how tired he seemed. When he glanced in our direction and saw me watching him, he quickly looked away, then sat staring at the floor. That's what confirmed it for me. I think Heidi always hoped he'd say he was sorry. But when I saw him in the courtroom that day, I knew that, even though he couldn't look me in the eyes, he wouldn't ever accept what he'd done. He was one of those people who could convince themselves of anything – that's why he was such a persuasive liar. If you believe the lies you tell yourself, it isn't very difficult to make other people believe them too.

I watched him as they read out the sentence for each of the counts he'd been found guilty of, and suddenly realised that he was a different man from the dad I remembered. He didn't look shocked, just broken and ... the only word I can think of to describe it is placid. I didn't feel sorry for him at all – I think the cold side of my character took over and I cut him off. He'd committed the crimes, now he was going to have to pay the penalty. That's just the way it works.

It was in the newspaper, the fact that he'd been found guilty of abusing his daughters and had been given a prison sentence. By the time he was convicted, I was the only member of the family who hadn't changed their name to

Harding. I didn't do it until about five years ago, when I wanted to give my children the legacy of having the same name as my mother and sisters. And although it did worry me a bit that I might be easily identifiable as his son, I wasn't as scared of other people as I had been when he was first arrested. What also helped was the fact that I had surrounded myself with real friends – people I trusted, rather than just drinking buddies and acquaintances – and none of them said anything to me about it.

When he went to prison, that was it for me. It was all over and done with; in the past.

Chapter Fifteen

Heidi

About a year after the trial, Liam told me one day – out of the blue, as far as I was concerned – that he wasn't happy with our relationship and wanted to start dating other people. I was still cautiously skirting around the crater created by this bombshell and had been spending a couple of days with Mum when I suddenly got a feeling that I had to go home. I didn't know why, I was just convinced something was wrong. When I got home, I found Liam in bed with a woman I didn't know, but who apparently went to the same gym as he did.

The kaleidoscope of emotions you experience when something like that happens is exhausting. I was hurt, angry, humiliated and completely devastated. Liam and I had been together for five years. I thought we were going to get married and be together forever. And he *was* a nice guy, but maybe not the strong character I really needed. I realised later that I hadn't treated him as well as I should have done, mostly by taking advantage of his attitude of being happy to do whatever *I* wanted to do, but also by shutting him out and rejecting his offers of support – when he asked if I wanted him to go with me to the trial, for example.

Breaking up with Liam hit me really hard, but one positive thing that came out of it was that I went back to live at Mum's for a while, during which time I got very close to Tom. Our relationship had improved tremendously after the trial – I think his being there at the court was a major turning point for me, because it felt as though he believed me at last. I started accepting his help when he offered it. And he was *really* good after I split up with Liam, often coming to find me on the many occasions when I left the house and went off on my own.

When I went back to the town where I had lived with Liam, I shared a house with a couple of wonderful friends, who did everything they could think of to cheer me up. Then I quit my job and, shortly afterwards, started another. Then, a year later, I was contacted by a recruitment agency and persuaded to go for an interview in London. By that time I was ready for my next adventure, so when I was offered the job, I accepted it. Then, a couple of months after I'd moved to London, my wonderful granddad – *his* dad – died. And not long after that, I met Fraser, the man who was to become my husband.

Chloe was the first of us to have a baby, a beautiful little boy. Four years later, Fraser and I had a little girl, who was just a few weeks old when Mum rang me at 8.30 one morning to tell me her dad was very ill. As soon as I put down the phone, I threw everything I might need into the car, strapped my baby into her car seat, told Fraser I'd be fine and that I didn't need him to come with me, and set off on the long drive to my grandparents' house. When I got there, Tom came out to meet me, to tell me that Granddad had passed away just five minutes before I arrived.

My mum's parents hadn't ever mentioned what had happened with my dad, not even after the court case. In fact, I had only ever talked to Granddad about it once, a couple of years before he died. He and Mum's partner, Ted, had come to stay with Fraser and me for a few days while Mum and Nan flew to the US to visit another family member who was ill. I drove them to the airport and when I got home again, Fraser, Granddad, Ted and I sat out in the garden and had something to eat.

Mum and Ted have been together for 16 years now. I was wary of him at first, but he's kind and always has time for our children and his own grandchildren. And as well as being about as different from my dad as it's possible for anyone to be, it was clear not long after he and Mum got together that his intentions towards her were good.

Later that evening, after Fraser and Ted had gone to bed and the house was quiet again, Granddad suddenly said to me, 'Why didn't you tell me? We were so close when you were a little girl. I'm really hurt that you didn't think you could talk to me about it. We went looking for him, you know, me and your uncle, after we found out what had happened. But we couldn't find him. Maybe it was just as well, because we were going to break his legs.'

I was horrified by what he said – hurting my dad was the last thing I'd have wanted him to do. But it was good to know he'd been concerned and hadn't just dismissed the whole thing, as I'd thought at the time. I suppose he and Nan were trying to be sensitive by not raising the subject unless I did. My mum's dad was a wonderful man, who had always been more like a dad to me than my own father had ever been. We could chat for hours and talked on the phone every lunchtime after I moved to London. So I was glad we'd had even that brief conversation about it, and I missed him terribly after he died. I still do.

It was about six months after Granddad's funeral when I had the same sort of feeling I'd had the time I rushed home to be with Liam and found him in bed with another woman. This time though, when I acted on my instinct, I hacked into Mum's Facebook account and found a message from Dad, asking, 'Can you tell me where my mum and dad are buried?'

'I've seen his message on Facebook,' I told Mum later that day. 'Why didn't you tell me about it? Have you replied to it?'

'No,' she said, 'and I'm not going to.'

'Why?' I asked. 'It's obvious that he's dying. Why wouldn't you answer him? He needs to know where his parents are buried.'

Although she was adamant that she didn't want to respond to his message herself, she didn't mind me doing so on her behalf, so I sent him the information he needed. But even though he didn't reply, I was convinced that something was happening, and I'm the sort of person who wouldn't be able to rest until I found out what it was. I contacted a cousin I hadn't seen or spoken to for a long time and asked her to meet me for coffee.

The reason I thought of that cousin, specifically, was because I knew she was close to her mother – my Uncle George's wife, Maureen – who had a reputation for knowing everything that was going on in the lives of all her friends and family members. And it turned out that I was right. After meeting up with my cousin a few times, I started asking her questions about my dad and she told me he was in a hospital not far from where Mum, Chloe and Tom all lived, and that he *was* dying, as I'd guessed from his message to Mum.

When I phoned the hospital, I spoke to a nurse, who said my dad would phone me back. It was only then that I really thought about what I was doing and realised I was quite scared and didn't want to talk to him after all.

'Well, I can't tell you anything unless I have his permission to do so,' the nurse said. 'I'll speak to him and see what he says.'

When she phoned me back, she said he'd given permission for her to talk to me. He was in the terminal stages of prostate cancer, and was being transferred to a hospice later in the week. 'He said he'd like to see you,' she added. 'But that if you did come, you'd have to "let sleeping dogs lie", and that you'd know what that meant.'

I did want to go and see him, but everyone told me not to, and in the end I allowed myself to be persuaded, which is something I still regret. I can't blame anyone else though, because I did have the opportunity to go to the hospice on the day he was transferred there from the hospital. I'd been to stay with Mum for a couple of days and was driving home with my baby daughter. I know it sounds stupid, but I had this vision in my mind of pushing him around the grounds of the hospice in a wheelchair, and of him taking that last opportunity to say ... I don't know what I wanted him to say. That he was sorry for what he'd done, I suppose. Or perhaps I thought he'd explain *why* he'd done it and then I'd finally understand.

To get to the town where the hospice was involved taking the long way home, which wasn't ideal with a baby in the car. But that's what I decided to do, and it wasn't until I was actually driving past the building that I suddenly thought, 'What am I doing? I must be mad even to think of taking *my* daughter to see a dying man who abused me and my sister when we were little girls.' Then I drove past the hospice without stopping, and cried for most of the long journey home.

Fraser and I were taking our baby away with us the next morning, to stay in a cottage in the countryside for a couple of days. Before we left, I phoned my dad's brother, George, and told him what I'd found out, but he didn't show any interest in going to see him. Then Maureen rang the following day, while we were at the cottage, to tell me that someone from the hospice had rung them and said they didn't understand why none of his family had visited him.

'She said only his friends have been to see him,' my aunt told me. 'Didn't you tell them what he did?'

'I didn't want to say anything because I didn't want them to change the way they look after him,' I explained.

'He's ill and I don't wish him any harm. But I'll phone the hospice now.'

'We just don't understand why you don't come, Heidi,' the nurse said when I rang.

'There *is* a reason,' I answered, swapping the phone to my other ear and opening my hand to allow the sweat on my palm to dry. 'It's difficult to talk about it, but I'm going to be very honest with you.' Then I told her, briefly, why I couldn't bring myself to visit my dying father.

'Heidi,' she said, very quietly, when I'd finished what I was saying, 'your dad died while you were talking. He said your name as he passed, and a word that sounded like clow.'

'That's what we call my sister,' I said. 'Chlo. It's short for Chloe.'

Then I locked myself in the bathroom, sat on the floor and sobbed.

I didn't understand why his death had affected me so badly. My reaction to it was different from anything I'd experienced before. I'd been heartbroken when my granddad died just six months earlier, but not even his death had hurt me the way this did. I felt disorientated too. Everything seemed strange – being a new mother and being away from home – and suddenly I didn't know where I fitted into the picture, or even what the picture was. So, after I'd phoned everyone who needed to know that he'd died, I phoned Lesley, because I thought I might be going just a little bit mad.

Lesley was brilliant, as she always was, and by the end of the phone call, I'd worked it all through and realised that I was just sad, and that was okay. I think the thing that made me saddest of all was having to accept that, now he was gone, I wasn't ever going to get what I'd always wanted from my father, although I didn't really know what that was. I just knew it was something that all my friends' fathers had given them when we were young, something they still give them now, as adults. Identity, perhaps. Or a sense of unconditional love. Or maybe just the knowledge that there's someone you can rely on who will always put your wellbeing above their own. In fact, someone who feels about you the way I've felt towards my child – and I know Fraser has, too – from the moment she was born.

While I was puzzling over my reaction to his death, I remembered how angry and upset I'd been with my friend Zoe when her abusive father died while we were at university. Suddenly I understood why she'd responded the way she did when she heard that he was dying. I rang her immediately and told her how sorry I was that I hadn't been more open-minded and supportive at the time. Fortunately, it hadn't adversely affected our friendship in the intervening years, and she accepted my apology and said she'd understood. It certainly taught me a lesson, though, and I realised that people are right when they say don't judge someone until you've walked a mile in their shoes.

When I phoned my Uncle George and told him his brother was dead, his reaction was purely practical. 'You won't want to organise the funeral,' he said. 'Your Auntie Maureen and I will do that.'

'Well … I don't know,' I answered. 'I just need some time to think about it.'

But I hadn't had a chance to think about it at all when I heard that they'd been to his flat.

'Your dad had nothing,' Maureen told me when she phoned me afterwards. 'He didn't have any money at all. You're probably going to have to pay for the funeral.'

'That's fine. Just let me know how much it is. But he must have had *some* stuff,' I said, trying to hide my irritation at the thought that, having had no contact with him for years, they'd taken it upon themselves to take control – on an organisational level, if not financially.

'No, he didn't have *anything* in the flat,' Maureen assured me.

It made me feel incredibly sad to think he'd died a lonely, broken man, living in a miserable, sparsely furnished flat. But at the back of my mind there was another thought – that something didn't seem to sit right. So I phoned the hospice, where they told me that everything he'd had when he was admitted to hospital had been given to my uncle and aunt, who had turned up there with a death certificate a couple of days after he died.

'We've got a note of it all,' the nurse told me. 'There was a wallet containing some cash, a couple of bank cards …'

George had told me specifically, 'He didn't have a bank card and when I phoned his bank they said there's no money, which is why I mentioned the fact that you might have to pay for the funeral.' Apparently, though, my uncle hadn't been telling the truth.

I got hold of a death certificate too, then went to the bank, where a clearly very embarrassed bank manager explained that, 'Your uncle said your dad didn't have any children.'

There was still just over £3,000 in an account, which I took to pay for the funeral – and because I didn't want my uncle and aunt to get their avaricious hands on it. Then, after I'd sorted things out at the bank, I tracked down the man who'd rented the flat to my father in exchange for the work he did as a handyman on some other properties. 'They told me they were his next of kin,' he said. 'I'm really sorry. I should have checked before I gave them the key to his flat. I'll go round there now and have a look.'

When he phoned me back a couple of hours later, he sounded shocked. 'They've cleaned him out,' he told me. 'His laptop's gone, and so has the jar of coins he collected. They've even unscrewed his telly off the wall and taken that.'

It didn't matter – none of us would have wanted anything he'd had. But what my uncle and his wife had done was wrong, and then they'd lied about it, too.

Tom said he would come to the funeral, and although at first Chloe didn't want to, she decided in the end that she would come too. They drove up with Mum, and Chloe's little boy, while I booked into a B&B with my baby, having once again insisted to Fraser that this was something I could do by myself.

Having slept badly throughout my childhood and on most nights as an adult until I met my husband, I now sleep soundly with him by my side. In fact, fear of the night-time only ever really returns if he's away for any reason; then I lie awake all night with my glasses on, waiting for something to happen. So, when I look back on it now, I realise that not accepting Fraser's offer to go with me was an indication of the fact that I wasn't in a good place mentally.

Mum stayed in the car throughout the funeral, to look after the children, and Chloe sat at the back of the room at the crematorium, crying, while Tom and I joined our dad's friends and fielded questions about why we hadn't been to see him before he died. I don't know what I'd expected the funeral to be like. Maybe not all that dissimilar to the way it was, although less surreal. He had obviously done what he always did after he came out of prison and made friends with people who made him feel better about himself by comparison. 'He was a great man, your dad,' they told us.

'He was always willing to help anyone,' said a woman who was probably about 80, but dressed like an 18-year-old.

'He taught my daughter to drive,' a man said, and I had to pretend I was coughing to try to disguise the sound of my shocked gasp.

'Will you do this reading?' another woman asked me, thrusting a dog-eared piece of paper into my hand. 'It's a great story, and so typical of your dad. It's about how he saved these cats and ...'

He'd served his time and made a new life for himself. And that was fine. But reading a story about something he'd done that proved what a great guy he was would definitely have been a step too far. So I handed the bit of paper back to her, made an excuse and, as nicely as I could, declined.

The wake after the funeral was held in a pub in town. But we went to a cafe instead – me, Mum, Chloe, Tom and the two children – and had tea and cakes. Then I set out on the long drive home, which ended up taking seven hours, which was more than enough time for me to realise what a huge mistake I'd made by insisting to Fraser that I could do it on my own. I was an emotional wreck, my baby was screaming, and I simply didn't know what to do. Even superheroes are defeated sometimes, I suppose.

The day after the funeral, Uncle George rang and said, 'We know what you've done, Heidi. How did you know the money was there?'

'I didn't,' I told him. 'I just knew you were lying to me, so I checked. And now it's in a holding account, which is where it's going to stay. What I don't understand is what made you think you had the right to take control. Tom should have been the person who went into his flat, not you and Maureen. And certainly not without consulting Tom first. His landlord said he had a jar full of pennies. Did you take that too?' I could feel myself getting angrier as I spoke.

It was quite likely that Tom wouldn't have wanted to go to the flat. Certainly none of us wanted any of his sad, meagre possessions or his money. But no one else had the right to barge in there and help themselves without even asking us. I suspected, too, that when they'd cleared it out, they'd found a lot more money than was in the penny jar. Unless he'd changed his habits after he came out of prison, he'd only have put his benefits money in the bank and would have kept a stash of undeclared earnings and cash from other shady deals closer to hand.

After I'd paid all the receipts for the funeral that my uncle sent me, I divided the few hundred pounds that remained between me, Chloe and Tom. And the next time I saw Uncle George – at my Uncle Harry's funeral about three years later – he blanked me. Which was fine by me.

Chapter Sixteen

Chloe

Life did eventually settle down after the trial. Mum's cancer treatment was successful, thank God. I split up with the mean boyfriend and started seeing a guy I'd known since primary school, who's my partner now and the father of our three children. Tom moved in with his girlfriend, Bridgette, and Heidi with Fraser; then they had children too. And *his* dad died at some point; I think it might have been after *he* came out of prison.

No one ever told me which prison he was sent to, and I didn't ever ask. We got a letter before he was released, stating that he wasn't allowed to try to talk to us or contact us in any other way, and that he mustn't enter the county we lived in for a certain period of time – I think it was something like a year. I suppose that was a condition of him being released early. When he came out, he apparently rented a flat in the neighbouring county, about 50 miles away from where I live now.

I was 22 by that time, had had my first child, and had changed my name to Harding. It was Heidi who suggested and paid for me to change my name. As my partner Jerry and I weren't married when our son was born, I was very glad that he wouldn't have *his* name. In fact, I can remember asking someone – I don't know who it would have been – if something could be added to the terms of his release from prison to say that he mustn't ever try to contact my child. But I don't know if that was done. Then I tried to forget about him, and never spoke to him again.

I think it was about three years ago when Heidi phoned me and said he was dying and in a hospice. 'He wants to see us,' she told me. 'Do you want to go?' She sounded very upset.

'Do you feel you *need* to go?' Jerry asked me when we talked about it later. And I realised that the answer was an emphatic 'No'. Although it might seem very harsh to say so, the thought that he was dying didn't bother me at all and I had no desire to see him.

'It will only bring up things I feel I've already dealt with,' I told Jerry.

'Fine,' he said, 'just do what you want to do. Heidi can see him if she wants to, but that doesn't mean you have to.'

I told Heidi not to go, though – I couldn't see why *he*'d even asked to see us. Then I didn't really think much more about it until a few days later, when Heidi rang again and said he'd died while she was talking to someone at the hospice on the phone.

Surprisingly perhaps, I cried when she told me he was dead. Not because I was sad about it; I wasn't at all. In fact, I was actually very relieved, because now that he was gone it felt as though we could all move on and forget about him. What *did* upset me was knowing that I would now never have a nice dad. That must sound like an odd thing to say, because, obviously, that had been the case before he died. But, somehow, his death made it seem more final.

I think I'd always thought it would all end the day he died. But it didn't, because Heidi and Tom decided they wanted to go to his funeral. As far as I was concerned, he'd been as good as dead for years and I couldn't see any point in going to his funeral to say goodbye. I wanted to show my support for Heidi and Tom, though, and I thought I might regret it if I didn't go. So I drove up with Mum, Tom and my little boy, who had turned four just a few weeks earlier. Heidi had had her baby by then, too, and Mum came so that she could look after the children while the three of us did whatever we decided we were going to do when we got there.

I knew it was going to be horrible, even if I did stay in the car as I planned to. The reality was even worse than I'd imagined. He'd obviously made a new life for himself in the town he'd moved to after he came out of prison, and when we went into the room at the crematorium where the service was going to be held, all his new friends were there.

It was obvious that none of them had any idea that he'd ever been in prison at all, let alone for having been found guilty of abusing his own daughters, so I could understand that they were grieving for his death. His brother George and George's wife Maureen were there, too, and maybe they were also genuinely upset, even though they hadn't got on with him while he was alive. What I couldn't understand, however, was the way our aunt and uncle behaved towards *us*, because, unlike his new friends, they *did* know what he'd done, yet they acted as though nothing had ever happened and his death was a great tragedy. They are horrible people – I don't think they ever really believed he'd done what he was found guilty of doing.

I think, for me, being greeted by his brother's wife as if she expected us to be upset was the last straw. That, and some woman telling a long story about *his* cats and how he always called them his babies, as though he was some really nice, sentimental, normal man with pets and friends and children, who his new friends were all determined to be pleasant to, despite the fact that they hadn't even bothered to go and see him when he was dying in a hospice.

His friends knew nothing about us, and it all felt embarrassingly fake. I kept thinking, 'Why am I here? Why am I bothering with this?' But when I glanced at Heidi to see if she was feeling the same way, she was talking to someone very calmly, as if it was all the most natural thing in the world. But it wasn't natural and I wasn't fine about it, as she seemed to be. I was angry, and getting angrier by the minute as I stood and watched Tom and Heidi talk to people I didn't want to talk to about aspects of *his* recent life that I didn't want to know anything about.

It turned out that his friends hadn't even known he had any kids, although Heidi said afterwards she thought some of them *did* know about what had happened – or, at least, his version of the events that had led to him going to prison, which I'm sure involved Heidi and me being to blame rather than it being due to anything *he* had done.

I didn't know anything about his life after he and Mum got divorced, and certainly not about anything he did after he'd served his sentence. Judging from the friends who came to his funeral, I imagine whatever he did continued to involve drinking.

When they started saying what a wonderful bloke he was, I had a sudden urge to shout, 'You don't know anything about him. He was a fucking arsehole!' I know it was wrong of me to feel that way, but at that moment I wanted him to have lived the last years of his life in a dismal bedsit, friendless and alone.

I think Heidi actually *wanted* to know about those last years before he died and what his new friends thought about him, but I didn't. It all just seemed fake and uncomfortable, like claiming a relationship with him that I didn't want to have. What I really wanted to do was make it clear to his friends in some way that I wasn't there for *him*, but for Heidi and Tom. I didn't say that, of course. In fact, his friends didn't really speak to me at all, perhaps because of the waves of angry hostility I must have been radiating in every direction.

What I also couldn't understand was why no one asked us, 'Where the hell have you been?' Surely they must all have been thinking it. But they just showed us photographs, which I didn't look at. And as I stood there, slightly outside the circle, watching Heidi, I kept thinking, 'Why are you doing this? We don't *need* to be here.' Then, eventually, I walked away and sat in the car for a while with Mum and the children.

I went back inside when the funeral service started, but I shook my head and pulled away to sit in the back row when someone tried to usher me to the front, where Heidi and Tom were already seated next to *his* brother and his wife.

Although I'd felt that I *should* go to the funeral service, I was determined that I wasn't going to sing any hymns or do anything else that might be interpreted as taking part in it in any way. What I actually wanted to do was stand up and walk out. But as I wasn't quite brave enough to do that, I just sat there at the back of the room, crying and oblivious to what was going on around me, thinking, 'Thank God he's dead. I should have stayed in the car, this is just a load of balls.'

When the service was finally over and we all went outside again, my head seemed to be full of questions: 'Why did they bring flowers? Why did I come?' However, it was probably just as well that I did go, because if I hadn't, I'd only have sat at home wondering what Heidi and Tom were doing and feeling guilty about not having gone with them.

As I understand it, the whole idea of funerals is that they're supposed to give people a chance to celebrate the life of someone they loved and to say goodbye to them. For me, it was a case of drawing a line under *his* life. And the only feeling I had about that was relief.

Chapter Seventeen

Tom

It must have been a couple of years after Dad went to prison
when I finally settled down, got a 'proper' job and stopped
spending all my money on alcohol and partying. In fact, I
met my partner Bridgette at work, about six years ago, and
a couple of years later I became a dad. I used to think about
my own dad a lot when my children were born.

I said no when Heidi asked if I wanted to go and see
Dad in the hospice. I tried to imagine the scenario – what
I'd say, how I'd be with him, what questions I'd ask him.
But I just couldn't picture it at all. Which was weird, because I'm usually quite good at imagining how things are
going to be in a particular situation. I think that was why I
decided not to go; that, and the fact that I didn't want to.
He'd had plenty of time and opportunities to make contact
with us.

There are no barriers with families – the members of
your family know who you are and there's no pretending.
I think that was why I was able to say to Heidi, 'I don't
want to see him.' My children were very young at the
time, so probably knowing what it feels like to be a dad
had some influence on my decision too. I can't imagine

doing *anything* that might even inadvertently harm my kids in any way, let alone ...

Now that I've got a partner and children of my own, as I get older and become more aware of what family life involves, I sometimes think about the things we didn't do when I was young that I want to do with my kids. Go on holidays, for example, and just spend time doing family stuff.

I thought everything was all right when I was a kid. At weekends and during the holidays, I often used to disappear for the whole day with my friends. You wouldn't let kids do that today, but in those days I don't think anyone told us not to do things, and we'd go off for long walks through the fields and down by the river. Some of the lads used to swim in the river, although I never did – I don't like not being able to see what's under my feet in the water.

I could swim, though. Dad taught me, by taking me to the local swimming pool one day and holding out a net for me to cling on to as he pulled me the length of the pool to the deep end, then yanked it away. I went under a couple of times, then swam to the side, and I was fine after that, because I knew I could stay afloat without any support.

He thought that was the best way for people to learn most things – hard and fast. Maybe he was right – I certainly learned to fend for myself soon enough when he left me alone in that flat when I was 17, with bills to pay and people banging on the door, trying to break in.

He taught me not to trust people, too, which was a lesson that was reinforced when I realised the father I'd always looked up to had been lying to me for all those months about what he'd done to my sisters.

Most people go through a phase when they're growing up of putting themselves first. For some people, like me, that involves going out drinking and having a good time; for others, it might be doing something else. For most people, however, that changes as they get older and become more mature. Whereas, for people like my dad, that mentality never alters and they remain at the centre of their universe until the day they die.

So I didn't go to the hospice before Dad died, but I did attend his funeral. I think I went so that I could draw a line under it all – I wanted to put an end to the fact of him being my father. And whereas, in my mind, seeing him in hospital would have been tied in with all the bad stuff, going to the funeral seemed like an opportunity to say goodbye to the other part of my dad, the part I want to remember, even now; the part that involved taking me fishing for the first time when I was six years old and doing all the other nice things we did together when I was a kid; the part that ended the day he got picked up by the police.

He was very good at making friends with people who made him feel like the 'top dog'. And judging from what his friends who came to his funeral said about him, that's what he'd done when he got out of prison. When we lived together in the flat, after he and Mum got divorced and before he left the country, he had a lot of friends like that, people who thought he was very intelligent and who looked up to him as if he was some sort of idol. The way they talked about him – saying how clever he was and that he could pick up any broken bit of machinery and make it work – coloured *my* view of him when I was a teenager. But you know what they say about idols with feet of clay.

The people at the funeral didn't know the truth about him, and it wasn't my place to tell them. I wasn't angry with him by that time. I wasn't ever as angry with him as Heidi and Chloe had been – he hadn't harmed me the way he'd harmed them. And what anger I did have for him just seemed to disappear when I knew he'd died.

The funeral was probably hardest of all for Chloe. She didn't want to go in the first place, but she tends to get emotionally drawn into stuff by the family, and feels she has to do things she doesn't want to do. On this occasion, particularly, she should have stuck to her guns, because she found it really difficult hearing his carefully selected group of friends, who were more broken than he was – superficially, at least – reminisce about him and say what a good guy he was. Heidi and I saw it through, though.

About three months later, I picked up his ashes and took them to a fishing spot on a little hidden beach we used to go to. It seemed like the right thing to do, to scatter them somewhere I thought the good part of my dad had been.

It was only a few weeks ago that I found out he actually did try to contact me when he came out of prison. Someone who used to work with him – a guy called Tony – had sent me a message at the time saying my dad had got in touch with him and asked him to ask me if I wanted to speak to him. 'I don't want to be involved myself,' Tony said in his message to me. 'But I'll put you in touch with your dad, if that's what you want. I've told him not to hold his breath, though. Sorry about this, Tom. I hope everything's good with you.'

Tony must have assumed I didn't want to know, which was true, but I didn't see the message at the time it was sent. I don't know what I'd have done if I had. I certainly wouldn't have wanted any face-to-face contact with my dad, but I might have got in touch with him through Facebook, just to find out what he wanted. Or maybe I wouldn't, because I was still quite angry with him, knowing what he'd done, and that he'd lied to me.

Everything that happened from the morning he got arrested and then phoned me when I was at my girlfriend's house was a lie. All the arguments we'd had about it had been fake. At the time I didn't know why Heidi would lie about it all, except that I knew she hated him. But I didn't really believe he would lie to me either. Whereas, in fact, he hadn't been truthful to me about anything.

So, no, I don't think I'd have made contact with him if I'd read Tony's message when he sent it. Maybe he already knew he was going to die. And when someone has done something really bad and only tries to get in touch with his family when he's dying, it seems to me that it's more likely to be for *his* sake than for theirs. That may sound harsh, but it's the way I felt when he was in the hospice, and the way I think I'd still feel if it was all happening now. One thing I *am* sure about is that he'd have wanted *something*. He certainly wasn't trying to get in touch to say he was sorry he'd lied, or sorry about the things he'd done to my sisters.

I used to think about him a lot, and wonder, 'What are you doing this morning?' But once he was in prison and out of the picture, I started building a better relationship with Chloe and Heidi. In fact, it was during the court case that we came back together as a family. Heidi and I had started getting on better even before then. I'd go and visit her when she was at university and we'd have proper conversations, which is something we'd never done before. We even talked about our dad. Not about what he'd done – I didn't want to know the details – but about how she felt. She would ask me how I felt about it all, too, and I'd give her my perspective. I think the drink helped when we had conversations like that!

When we were younger, as kids, I'd always had a closer relationship with Heidi than with Chloe, because we were just two years apart in age and had forged a bond before Chloe was born, when I was five and Heidi was seven. Chloe and I are close now, though. We don't have deep conversations. Talking about our feelings is something that doesn't come naturally to either of us, possibly even less so for Chloe than for me. But we've got a bond, and that's what really matters.

One day, when my children are old enough to understand, I'll tell them everything – as long as Heidi and Chloe will let me. Despite the fact that talking isn't something *we* tended to do as a family, I do talk to my own children, and I expect they'll ask about their granddad one day – who he was and what he did. I don't want to hide it from them; I think that would be the worst thing I could do. But I won't tell them until they're at least 16, when they should know everything they need to know about keeping safe. I want my children to be aware that although you might think you can trust someone, you have to remember that everyone has secrets, no matter who they are. That doesn't mean you can't trust *anyone*, you just need to be conscious of that fact, so that you exercise some caution.

Another reason for waiting until they're older is that I want them to have had plenty of time to form strong bonds with their aunts and to be mature enough to understand that what happened to them doesn't in any way change the people they are.

I've been working in the same job for about 15 years now, although I'm just about to change track and move into a different area of work, as soon as I finish the college course I'm doing one evening a week. It was probably the counselling I had a few months ago that helped me focus my mind and decide what I really want to do.

I initially went for counselling to talk about a gambling problem I'd developed, but I started talking about my past. I hadn't expected it to come up at all – I only actually talked about the gambling in the first session, then spent the next nine dealing with all the other stuff.

The counselling certainly seems to have sorted out the gambling, which isn't a problem anymore, but with regard to the other issues – that might be a question Bridgette would be in a better position to answer! I hadn't been aware before I had counselling of feeling that I needed to talk about what had happened, and I wasn't conscious of feeling any different after it. What I did find interesting was that I began to remember more about the past, and to make links that I hadn't previously made. The counsellor didn't really say very much during the sessions. I created some timelines, which helped unlock some of the memories and made me understand why I did certain things that I hadn't ever understood before, because I was just a kid when I did them.

I suppose the answer to the question, 'Was the counselling helpful?' would have to be, 'Yes – if only in small ways.' For example, I've always felt I should have *known*. But when the counsellor asked me, 'Did you feel guilty about not seeing anything?' I realised that the answer to *that* question was, 'Not really, because I *didn't* see anything.' I think I would feel very guilty if I'd known what he was doing and hadn't acted on that knowledge, or if I'd chosen not to notice. But that wasn't the case.

I think Mum feels bad about it, though, and I can understand why – now that I'm a parent myself and it nearly kills me every time something hurts my children in any way.

It was only recently, when I was thinking about telling my story, that I even considered the possibility that my parents split up because Mum knew – or had suspicions about – what he was doing. I don't think she did, although I do think she feels that she *should* have known. But even today, when child abuse is talked about much more openly than it was even just 10 or 15 years ago, how many women would ever think that their partner might be abusing his own children?

Ultimately, everyone has their own way of dealing with things. Some people think there's a right way and a wrong way to do everything. But that's not the case. There are lots of different ways, and different people can have completely different perspectives about what appears to be the same issue. I know Chloe is all about keeping it all inside and not talking about it, and that seems to work for her – for now, anyway. Whereas Heidi wants it out in the open. I think Heidi feels that talking about it helps her come to terms with it, and to understand it – as much as one can understand something like that. I suppose I'm somewhere between the two. I'll talk about it if I need to for any reason, and I won't pretend it didn't happen, but, otherwise, I'm happy to turn my back on the past and look towards the future.

Chapter Eighteen

Chloe

I wasn't really angry about the abuse itself, perhaps because I hadn't known when it was happening that it was wrong. What I *was* angry with *him* about, however, was the fact that he'd destroyed our family and deprived me of a real dad. It probably sounds peculiar, but I think I'll always resent the fact that no one will ever say to me, 'Wasn't your dad lovely?'

I was angry with my mum, too, for a while after *he* died. I used to think, 'Why didn't she know? *I* would know if someone was abusing my child.' Then I realised that when you love someone, it wouldn't even cross your mind that they could do something like that, particularly not at that time, when child abuse wasn't talked about as openly as it is now. When we were young, I don't think my mum knew that there are apparently 'normal' men who abuse their own children, so I can understand why she wouldn't have believed that it was something the man she loved was capable of doing.

That's why it's so important to me that Jerry is such a good father – he's the dad to my children that I didn't ever have. We've been through some difficult times, I suppose most couples have. But even when we split up for a while, when our first child was small, he made sure he saw him every day. The fact that he's a really good dad is one of the reasons I'll always try to work things out with him. Although we have some different ideas about childcare, I *know* he wouldn't ever abandon his children, or do anything that might harm them in any way – and I say that as someone whose own experiences have taught me to be deeply suspicious of *everyone*. In fact, I never allow anyone except Jerry and my mum to look after my children, even for just a few minutes.

I've told my eldest son that no one, not even Mummy and Daddy, should touch his body unless he's hurt. What's also really important to me is that he knows he can talk to me about anything. He's around the age now that I was when the first incident I can remember occurred.

My whole purpose in life is to love and protect my children. Knowing they're well looked after and happy is what makes *me* happy. I can't even begin to understand how *he* could have done what he did to any child, let alone to his own daughters. I know I won't ever understand it, or excuse it. There are times when we all justify to ourselves the reasons why we haven't done something we should have done or *have* done something we shouldn't. But not even the most forgiving person could excuse what *he* did.

There's no doubt that what he did to me when I was a little girl damaged me emotionally; I realise that now. But

I think it's worse for Heidi, because, unlike me, she did eventually have some understanding of what he was doing to her. She has a different kind of anger towards him. Maybe starting to realise that was what helped to improve the relationship I have with her.

I was very angry with Heidi for a very long time after she read the secrets in my diary and showed them to Mum, while all the time denying she knew anything about them. We used to have terrible fights after that. I can remember one occasion, when we were a bit older, I'd used something of hers without asking – probably her hair straighteners or make-up – and in the fight that followed, I ended up pinning her against the wall. It really felt as though my blood was boiling and that I hated her so much I could have killed her.

Poor Heidi. She did what she thought was the right thing to do at the time. And she probably *was* right, but I just couldn't see it, or even begin to understand why she'd done it, until many angry years later. When I was a child, I felt as though I was being controlled by *him*. Then, after Heidi lied to me about having opened my locked diary, read the secret words I'd written in it and shown them to someone else, *she* seemed to take control of my life and to push me into a situation that was far worse than the one I'd been in before, which had been embarrassing but which *he* had made me believe was almost normal.

It wasn't until Heidi went to university that things started to get a bit better between us. They improved even more after the court case, then again when I had kids, and finally when *he* died and it felt as though that part of my life had ended: *he* had gone – not absconded this time, but gone for good – and it was finished.

Perhaps, for me, the major change occurred when I had my first child and suddenly decided, 'I'm going to have my own life now.' Although I did get a degree recently, I hadn't ever had 'professional' ambitions like Heidi. In fact, the only thing I'd ever really wanted was a family of my own. So from that point on, my focus was almost entirely on my son, and then, subsequently, on my second and third children too. From the moment my first baby was born, I stopped caring about *him* and what he'd done to me, because anything I *had* felt about him had been completely overridden by what really mattered – my own family.

Heidi was really good when my first child was born. She did my baby shower and was there for me every step of the way, and we became much closer. We didn't ever talk about what had happened. In fact, it wasn't until I agreed to write about the few childhood experiences I can remember that I told her, for the first time, how angry I was with her when she read my diary and how much I hated her because of what she did. It was the first time, too, that I had ever thought about it from her point of view. Which is when I realised that she wasn't just being nosy and controlling: she did what she did because she was trying to protect me, and she didn't ever understand the impact her actions had on me.

The few people who know about what *he* did to me always say there must have been more incidents than the ones I've described. And I suppose they're right. I think the reason I remember those specific incidents is because of the triggers associated with them – seeing *Thunderbirds* on the TV again, for example, or a memory popping into my head one day when I was at Mum's house and sat on the sofa that is still in exactly the same position as it was when *he* lived there and abused me on it.

Once, when I was still working in the supermarket, a man who came through my till smelled really strongly of Brut, and I had to put my light on and almost run to the toilet. *He* used to wear Brut and the smell of it that day threw me instantly into a state of panic. All I could think about was getting away from it before I was sick. It's for the same reason that I can't bear the smell of cigarette smoke and beer, and why I get agitated and anxious when people around me are drinking. I don't know what the specific link is with alcohol, and I do try not to let it upset me, but I hate it, to the point of giving poor Jerry a hard time if he has more than just one beer.

When something does trigger a memory, I don't just sit there and think about it. I get up and start doing something else to take my mind off it. In fact, if I'm upset for some reason or want to think something through, I'll often go outside and sit in the car for ten minutes. I solve most of my problems in the car, and it's where I cry when I need to. I suppose it's the one place where I feel safe enough to be able to sit and think things through and release the stress that builds up when I've been worried about something. I need that outlet, because I can't talk about problems like Heidi does. She and I deal with things differently. Maybe my method isn't as effective as hers, but it works for me – at least, it has done so far. She does have a better understanding of everything that happened though, and of the timeline of events, which I can't make head or tail of. The counselling she's had has helped with that.

I was very young when our parents divorced and no one told me what was going on after Tom left home to live with Dad, so I don't know what it was like from his perspective. In fact, when Heidi first asked Tom and me to help her write this book, I wondered why Tom agreed to do it, because he hadn't been abused by *him*, so I didn't think he'd have much to add to the story. Then I read some notes he'd written and they made me cry, which was when I began to realise how hard it had actually been on him. And once I began to think about that, I became conscious of the fact that I didn't really know Heidi's side of the story either, because I'd interpreted her actions at the time only in terms of the impact they had on *me*.

It's strange to think that three children can be brought up by the same parents, live in the same household, even share the same bedroom – as was the case for Heidi and me – and still be completely oblivious to what's happening right under their noses. No wonder Mum didn't know about it either.

I don't remember what my relationship was like with *him* when I was very young. Apparently, we were quite close – closer than Heidi ever was with him, according to what she's always said. I know I grew very close to my mum after Heidi found my diary. I see Mum every day now and she still supports me in lots of ways. I think Heidi's relationship with her is different, because Heidi moved away, and maybe also because Mum is a bit like me in that we both tend to say things without thinking.

I do regret some of the things I've said in anger to Heidi in the past. I wish I hadn't told her I thought she was controlling, because it was a hurtful thing to say, and she keeps things like that in her head forever. But a lot of it's probably just the older sibling/younger sibling thing. I've heard other people say that they feel like confident, competent adults in their normal daily lives, then slip back into their childhood roles as soon as they see their siblings.

The fact that Heidi and I mostly communicate on the phone rather than face to face makes our relationship more difficult too, because when she inadvertently says something that makes me feel as though she thinks I'm still six years old, I bite without thinking. Then, whatever I've said just hangs there between us until the next phone call, which might not be for some time if we've really offended each other. If we didn't live so far away, I could say I was sorry the next time I saw her, which is something I'm not very good at saying on the phone. What I also sometimes tend to overlook is that when I *do* say something critical, I might forget about it as soon as I've put the phone down, whereas Heidi won't, because she'll think I really meant it – which I might have done in the moment when I said it, but only because I was cross.

So maybe one of the things that contributing to this book has made me realise is that I should think about my actions a bit more. I don't suppose I'll get any better at apologising for the sort of sibling things I might say in the heat of the moment, but I could work on phoning back and saying I'm sorry. What's even more important to me, however, is that Heidi and Mum don't feel bad because they think they could have done something to stop what *he* was doing to me. *He* was very good at hiding it, and I would hate Heidi to spend the rest of her life thinking, 'Why didn't I do this or that?'

When I first started writing this book, I didn't want my partner, Jerry, to read it, and I didn't want to read Heidi's part either. She's been incredibly brave to do what she's done, but I didn't think I'd be able to bear to know all the details of what happened to her, even though I would like to understand why she looked in my diary. Now I'm coming to the end of telling my story, I think I will read Heidi's chapters after all. I need to understand her perspective on what happened.

Ultimately, though, what *he* did, and the chain of events that was triggered by Heidi reading my diary, are in the past. Nothing can change what happened. It's just life. All you can do is get on with it the best way you can. We always assume other people's lives are easier than ours, but I don't suppose they are. I expect everyone has something they have to battle with. And not everyone has three beautiful children and a lovely partner, like I do. So, really, I'm lucky.

Chapter Nineteen

Heidi

When Tom told me he'd gone back to the crematorium to get the ashes, I went to his house and asked if I could see them. I don't know what sort of container I'd expected them to be in, but certainly not a plastic jar, like a blacked-out, old-fashioned sweet jar. I suppose Dad's brother, George, chose that option when he was organising the funeral because it was the cheapest.

It took a lot of strength to do what Tom did – take three buses carrying a jar that was full to the brim of his dad's ashes so that he could bury it on a beach where the two of them used to go fishing. I was glad he did that.

It took me about 18 months to get over our dad's death, although I think a large part of that grieving process was related to the fact my granddad, my dad and my husband Fraser's mum – who was a really lovely lady – all died within the space of a year. Those events in themselves would have been bad enough. What made it even worse was the fact that it was my maternity year, which should have been one of the happiest times of my life.

I was certainly affected by Dad's death though, which was odd, because I'm sure that if I'd still known him when he died, I'd still have hated him, judging by how sick and angry I felt when Tom showed me a photograph of him that had been taken not long before he died and that was found propped up on a shelf in his flat. But I suppose you can't hate anyone with the same degree of intensity forever, and time does make you forget. Or at least it takes the edge off some of the sharp corners of your feelings, because I don't think I'll ever forget what he did to me or to Chloe.

People sent cards and said how sorry they were when my granddad and Fraser's mum died. But no one said anything about Dad, except things like, 'I expect you're glad he's gone,' or, 'He got what he deserved,' or even, in the case of one really close friend who knew about the abuse I'd suffered as a child, 'You can get over it now and get on with your life.' And although I think Chloe was glad he'd gone, I didn't feel like that at all. For me, his death just brought more pain and often when I thought about it, which I did a great deal during the 18 months after he died, I didn't feel very well. However, I think the real reason for my distress during that time was because I was sad for what he'd deprived me of, rather than because he was gone. In fact, I think it was a real turning point in my life, when quite a lot of things changed.

Everything that happens to us throughout our lives – particularly when we're children – has an effect on our perspective on all sorts of things. For example, being abused by my father made me absolutely terrified when I found out that the baby I was having was a girl. I was very sick for the first few weeks of the pregnancy, which was part of the reason why I was so convinced I was carrying a boy. So when Fraser and I were offered the opportunity to find out the sex at the 20-week scan, it seemed to me to be almost a formality. Even so, I was surprised by how nervous I felt when the day came, and by how shocked and upset I was when they said, 'It's a girl.'

It took six weeks for me to come to terms with the fact that I was going to be responsible for a little girl, and during that time I worried about *everything*. How could I possibly protect her when there would be so many things I wasn't going to be able to control? I knew I wouldn't be able to let her go to someone's house for day care, for example, because although the carer herself would have been checked, what about 'Uncle Bob', who drops round from time to time? And what would happen when my little girl went to nursery? Obviously, it would have to be a nursery that employed exclusively female staff, although even that wouldn't be a fail-safe, by any means. I know bad things happen to little boys, too, but I could identify more easily with a little girl and, in my mind, my daughter would be like me – or, worse still, like Chloe, who had needed protection that I hadn't managed to give her.

Fraser understood my concerns, to a point. However, most of them I kept to myself, until it all came to a head when I was a bridesmaid at my best friend's wedding, just three weeks before I was due to give birth. I was so tired by that time that all the emotion of the wedding tipped me over the edge, and I spent the next day crying. The thought that kept going round and round in my head was that, in just a few days' time, Fraser and I were going to be responsible for the tiny female person who would be born into a world where some men – and women – abuse children. I knew she would be safe with Fraser – his very strong sense of right and wrong is one of the reasons I love him – but we couldn't keep her safe at home forever.

I fell in love with my little girl from the moment I first saw her. The problem was, the massive emotional response I had to her made me very wary, because I'd adored Chloe from the day *she* was born too. Chloe had become my best friend, then I'd let her down and she'd hated me – for reasons I didn't understand at all until very recently. So what if I got really close to my daughter and then I let *her* down too?

What I hadn't thought about during all those weeks of worrying was how wonderful it was going to be, spending time with my little girl as she grew from baby into toddler into full-blown child, playing dressing-up games with her and doing all the other things I wish I'd been able to do when I was her age. Or how much pleasure I would derive from watching her interact with Fraser, and from knowing what an amazing relationship the two of them have.

My dad often used to laugh at me and call me stupid. He did it to Mum as well, criticising and belittling everything she did or tried to do. But *she* was the one who worked from dawn to dusk and beyond in the pub, while he played the role of convivial host, drinking with the customers and never lifting a finger to help her. And *he* was the one who ultimately destroyed the business, not only by – almost literally – liquidating the assets, but also by mishandling the finances Mum was forced to hand over to him when she was ill and had to go into hospital.

After all those years of being ridiculed and abused, it took me a long time – and many hours of counselling – to build up my self-esteem to a functioning level.

I know I've often said the wrong thing to Chloe, because I don't always know when it's a good idea to stop trying to micromanage everything and leave people alone to make their own choices. I think one of the reasons why I've sometimes been bossy and controlling – verbally, at least – is because I always seemed to want more for her than she wanted for herself. That's why I was very proud of her when, at the age of 18, she took her share of some money our paternal granddad left to us when he died and bought a plane ticket to France, where she'd got herself a job.

Chloe and I had a very up-and-down relationship for quite a few years after I read her diary and our dad was arrested. I've got a fairly vivid imagination, and what I'd imagined would happen was that she would turn to me for support. So I was completely taken by surprise when she reacted in the opposite way, and not only didn't want anything to do with me, but got the support and cuddles she needed from Mum instead, which is what I had always wanted.

I was really angry with Chloe when he was arrested that first time and she wouldn't give a statement – I thought she was being selfish and was only concerned about the impact she thought it might have on her. Now, though, I can't believe I didn't realise that she was just 11 years old and she was frightened. To Chloe, it must have felt as if, having been controlled by him, she was now being controlled by the people who wanted her to talk about something that was humiliating and embarrassing, something she desperately wanted to remain a secret. At the time, though, I already felt terrible because I thought I'd let her down, so her response seemed like confirmation of the fact that I really had failed to protect her.

A friend at university once said to me, 'I don't understand, Heidi. How did your mum not see it?' And I know that's a question Mum still asks herself. All I can say is: I was *looking* for it and I still missed it – for at least *three years*. Three years of him doing that to my little sister. Even now, I still can't think about that without crying. I don't think I'll ever stop feeling that I let her down, or stop asking myself, 'What more could I have done?' Because there's no arguing with the fact that if I *had* done things differently – if I hadn't believed him when he told me I had to keep the secret otherwise Mum would be hurt and our family would break up – he wouldn't have had the opportunity to do what he did to Chloe. And if Chloe hadn't been abused by him, and if all the things that happened as a result of that abuse hadn't happened, she would have been a very different person today, in terms of self-confidence and self-belief. As I would have been too, of course, if he hadn't done what he did to me.

I was very proud of Chloe when she got a degree recently, and I hoped it would make her realise that she can do whatever she sets her mind to doing. In fact, it was while she was working towards her degree that Nan told me one day, 'It's time to stop now, Heidi.'

That's when I finally understood that if I took a step back and stopped trying to support Chloe, she wouldn't collapse in a heap on the floor. What she really wants, certainly at this stage in her life, is the same thing she's always wanted: a family of her own. And whereas counselling has made me stronger, Chloe's strength comes from her children, who she and her partner are doing an amazing job of bringing up.

With Tom, the situation was very different. Tom was close to his dad when we were young and I think, for several years, he couldn't understand why I hated him so much. Perhaps that was part of the reason why we used to fight all the time before our parents got divorced and Tom went to live with him. I can remember one occasion, when I was in our parents' bedroom trying to stop my brother coming in, he pushed the door so violently it broke off its hinges and crashed down on top of me. Another time, he threw a dinner mat at me, like a Frisbee, and I picked up one of his dad's steel-capped boots and hit him with it. But although the fights we had were very physical and full of anger, he was my brother and I'd have done anything to protect him, just as I would have done for Chloe. I was so glad when we started to talk to each other again, and had the sort of relationship I'd always really wanted to have with him.

It was a relationship that sometimes involved me lending him money – which he always paid back – or helping him in other ways, such as the time when I was at university and working one evening when he phoned me from London en route to catch a ferry to France.

'I fell asleep on the Tube,' Tom told me, and I could hear the panic in his voice. 'I'm going to miss the ferry. Can you stop it for me?'

'I can do a lot of things,' I said, half-amused and half-pleased that he'd asked for my help, 'but I don't think I can stop a ferry. I'll give it a go, though.'

I rang the ferry port and explained that my brother had fallen asleep on the Tube and had ended up on the other side of London to where he needed to be. 'I know this isn't possible,' I said to the clearly bemused person who had answered the phone, 'but I told him I'd ask. Is there any chance that you could stop the ferry leaving until he gets there?'

They couldn't, of course. But it all worked out well in the end for Tom – as things so often do – because after I'd rung maybe 30 B&Bs, none of which would take my credit card (perhaps wisely, Tom didn't have a credit card himself at that time in his life), I found a place and booked a room. And not only did it turn out to be really nice, but after he'd had a good night's sleep, the owner cooked him a huge breakfast, then drove him to the ferry port himself.

Tom's a really wonderful person and a much better man than his dad could ever have been. You can certainly tell that he's been on an emotional journey and that he knows now what he wants, and what he wants to do. Perhaps it has helped him to know what sort of person he *didn't* want to be.

One of the things I respect most about my brother is the fact that he was there for Chloe and me during the trial, sitting quietly outside the courtroom every day, then coming in for the sentencing, not because that was something he would ever have wanted to do, but because we told him we wanted him there. But despite everything that has happened, and the terrible truth he'd learned about his dad, he still did the right thing by going to get his ashes and scattering them on a beach where there were only happy memories of him. I have a lot of love and respect for Tom for doing that. It can't have been easy for him.

In some ways, things were easier for me with Tom than they were with Chloe, because Tom doesn't hesitate to tell you – or simply walk away – when he thinks you're trying to control him. In fact, when he went through a bad phase not very long ago and I told him, 'I know there's something wrong. I want to help you. I want to be there for you,' his response was, 'Heidi, will you *please* just leave me alone. I don't want to talk to you about it.'

Maybe it's surprising that it's taken so long for it to dawn on me that I might not make things very easy for the people close to me – that maybe I don't know everything after all! What I do know now, however, is that I need to take a step back and not insist on taking charge or trying to help people when they don't really need or want my help.

Maybe it was realising – even subconsciously – at a very young age that life can be very confusing and frightening that made me always want to protect and take care of Chloe and Tom. I know I overdid it sometimes, and that I still do. But, in a way, I was my own worst enemy, because I was so determined to be strong for them, and for Mum, that I didn't ever let them see that beneath my capable and resilient superhero exterior there is another part of me that is still a very vulnerable, anxious little girl.

I've had a lot of counselling from Lesley over the last 20 years, and she was very supportive of my long-held hope one day to write a book about our story. So I feel as though I've worked through most of what happened. Now the story has been written, I can close the book, put it on a shelf, and move on with my life.

Chapter Twenty

Mum

It almost makes me feel guilty to say it now, but I loved my husband. We got on really well and had a lot of good times together in the early days. Otherwise I wouldn't have stayed. He didn't drink when I first met him. We might have the odd glass of wine, but we never drank until we were silly. And then he changed.

Heidi adored her dad when she was young. He used to carry her around on his shoulders, the way dads do, and she always wanted to be with him. Chloe adored him too, and would climb all over him when they were playing. Then, slowly, things started to change. Chloe would still ride on his back when he got down on all fours, like a dog or a donkey. But she began to pull his ears and hair while she was doing it. Not gently; it was as if she was really trying to hurt him. She'd do it when they were sitting on the sofa watching TV, too – suddenly reach up and yank his ear as hard as she could. I didn't know why she was doing it at the time. When I look back on it now, however, I wonder if it was all part of it – I just don't know.

Then, as Heidi got a bit older, she *hated* him. This was before he started being so horrible to me. My mum used to say that she couldn't understand why Heidi seemed to hate him so much. I didn't know either, so we decided it must just be because she was a teenager. Some young people do go through phases when they're growing up, don't they? Then they come out of them and everything's all right again. And because Heidi and I did everything together at that stage and she always wanted to be with me anyway, I assumed it must just be something girls do.

We worked very hard when we took over the pub. At least, I did, while he played the role of 'mine host'. I've seen the same thing in quite a few other pubs since then, including our local here, where the husband stands behind the bar chatting with the customers and the wife works almost constantly in the kitchen. Then, after we left the pub, I went *out* to work instead.

I divorced him because he was going out drinking every night, then coming home and yelling at me until three o'clock in the morning. Night after night, he'd put his hands around my neck, gripping me so tightly I couldn't move, and push my head against the wall, or the pillow if I was in bed, with his face so close to mine I'd be showered in his spit as he shouted at me. It was incredibly frightening. And exhausting too, because even when I hadn't slept, I still had to get up in the morning and go to work.

I didn't know what it was all about or why he suddenly started accusing me of sleeping with every man we ever came across – his brothers, neighbours, men working in the shops we went into, even colleagues he had worked with years before. He was so jealous and convinced his suspicions were right, he used to drive around town looking for me when I came out of work or if I'd been shopping. But if he did see me waiting at a bus stop, he wouldn't stop and give me a lift home. Having satisfied himself that I *was* where I was supposed to be, he'd turn around and drive back on his own. I could have understood why he started making all those accusations if I'd ever shown any inclination to be unfaithful, even slightly. But I hadn't. So I just didn't know where it was all coming from.

When I decided, after 20 years of marriage, that I'd had enough and went to see a solicitor about getting a divorce, she told me, 'There's basically nothing we can do unless there's blood on the wall.' In other words, they couldn't do anything about his behaviour unless I could prove that he was beating me up. But he wasn't; he didn't ever hit me. What he did that evening after we'd been to the solicitor, however, was hold me by the neck, the way he always did, and shout at me, 'I know where you and Heidi went today. I know you've been to see a solicitor. I pretended to be an electrician and went to his office after you'd been there.' He sounded quite mad, and what he was yelling at me didn't make sense anyway, because the solicitor wasn't a man at all, but a very nice woman called Mrs Hendry.

In the end the grounds for divorce – which he agreed to – were that the marriage had irretrievably broken down. He was in the pub when the divorce papers were served on him – at least his drinking meant we always knew where to find him! But he wouldn't move out of the house while the divorce was going through. He just carried on his life as normal. Even after it was finalised, he refused to leave. In the end I had to get a court order, and when the judge told him he had seven days to leave the property, he said, 'I'm very sorry, Your Honour, but I won't be able to leave in seven days.' When the judge asked him why, he didn't have a reason, so he had to do it. And when he finally did move out, he took my son with him – basically so that he'd be able to get a council flat. I was devastated when Tom told me he was going to go with him.

I was the one who bought the diaries for the girls. When I was a girl, I didn't ever have anything private – my mum was always going in and out of my room, to clean it and make the bed, so that's why I bought them diaries with locks. When I look back on it now, I think, 'What a *stupid* person you were not to have looked at what they wrote.' I think I'll feel guilty forever about that, about Chloe especially. But I wanted them to have the privacy I'd never had, and to be able to write about their own private thoughts, knowing that no one else would read them.

Then, one day, Heidi said to me, 'There's someone I want you to meet, Mum.' I don't know who I thought she was taking me to see – a friend of hers, I suppose. Anyway, she met me after work the next day – I think I finished at two o'clock in those days – and we sat outside Boots and had a prawn sandwich. Then she took me round to these offices, where I thought her friend must work.

It was only when we went upstairs and she introduced me to Lesley that I started to wonder what the hell was going on. And I was even more apprehensive when Lesley said, 'Heidi's got something to tell you. Do you want to tell your mum, Heidi? Or do you want me to do it?'

'I'll tell her,' Heidi said.

It was unreal – it felt as though there'd been an explosion in my body and I just couldn't believe what she was saying.

I remember that I said, 'Right. So what do we do now, Lesley? How do we deal with this?'

Heidi told me later she was really hurt, because she'd expected me to break down. I don't know why I didn't, except that, when anything bad happens – your child has an accident and falls off their bike, for example – I seem to have the opposite of an adrenaline rush. So instead of running towards the accident, I tend to stop and think about what to do, because I don't want to start panicking and do the wrong thing. I think another factor was also that I didn't want to break down in front of Heidi: as a mum, I always feel I have to be strong.

Lesley was amazing, so kind and good to us all. I think she told the police and social services that afternoon and they started working it all out.

No one said anything to him for a while – the police wanted to get the girls' statements first. But poor Chloe! They sat her in this chair and said, 'Right, there's a camera there, one over there, and another here. So now we're going to talk to you ...' It was hardly surprising she ran away and locked herself in the toilet; it was awful. She thought what had happened was private and no one would know, because although she'd written about it in her diary, she'd stuck photos over it.

I still don't know exactly what it said. It was Heidi who read it, not me, although I've always thought I should have looked – then I'd have been the one to find out.

'The only reason I read it,' Heidi told me afterwards, 'was because I was *looking* for any sign that he was doing something to her. Whereas you didn't know there was anything to look *for*. That's the difference.'

I still feel bad about it, though.

I don't know what happened to the diary – I think I must have burned it. I know I didn't want it in the house afterwards. I was afraid that if anything happened to me, someone might find it – maybe even my mother – and I wouldn't have wanted anyone else to see it.

It wasn't until after I found out about what had been happening that I remembered when Heidi visited me in hospital once. She must have been about 10 or 11, and when she sat down on the chair beside the bed she said, 'Mum, I want to tell you something.'

'What?' I asked. 'What is it, Heidi?' But, at that moment, *he* came in with Chloe and she didn't say anything else.

I still often think about that and wonder, 'Was she going to tell me what he'd done to her?' I don't suppose she remembers now either – I just wish I'd asked her about it later. But there are lots of things in life that one can look back on and think, 'I wish I'd done this or that.'

There was another occasion, after we were divorced but before I knew anything about what had happened, when he phoned up and said he wanted to take Chloe out for Sunday lunch. When I told Chloe she said, 'I'll only go if Tom comes as well,' which I thought was a bit strange, but then I decided it was just because she was missing Tom and wanted to see him too. It certainly didn't cross my mind that there was any sinister reason for it. I think I did tell him what Chloe had said, but I can't remember whether or not she went to have lunch with him. So many of the memories are so awful, you just want to get rid of them.

We were very frightened before Tom told me his dad had gone abroad – I certainly wouldn't have ruled out the possibility that he would break into the house and try to harm us. So, every night, before I went to bed, I used to put a broom and a chair by the front door to jam the letterbox shut, in case he carried out the threat he'd often made and tried to set the house on fire while we were asleep in our beds.

I had been very worried about Tom, too, when he was still living with his father. Fortunately, he had a girlfriend whose parents were very supportive and he often used to stay there. After his dad left the country, Tom lived on his own in the flat for a while, until there was an attack on the front door by someone with a machete. I think I was in hospital at the time, with breast cancer, because I can remember having to arrange for someone to pick up the dining table and chairs so that Tom could come home and sleep in the dining room.

When I answered the phone one day, someone said, 'I need George's phone number and my cousin's address.' I didn't recognise his voice, but when I asked, 'Who *is* this?' he said, very coldly, 'You *know* who this is.' A few days later, he gave himself up.

The girls didn't want me to go into the courtroom while they were giving their evidence. But when Lesley offered to come with me, I did go in to hear him give his, and be questioned by Heidi's barrister. It was the first time I'd seen him in a few years and I was shocked by the way he looked. He was wearing a black sweatshirt and had a beard and greasy, swept-back hair; he looked horrible. His voice was a lot gruffer too. He'd been in prison for quite a while before the trial, so he can't have been drinking at that time, although he looked as though he had been.

It was surreal, seeing him sitting there looking so dishevelled and hearing him say things like, 'I still love my wife,' and, 'I wouldn't ever have done any of the things I've been accused of. I wouldn't have lifted a finger to harm any of my children.' When he said he still loved me, I can remember looking at him and thinking, 'What do you mean? What a *stupid* thing to say.' Then he was questioned by Heidi's barrister about when the children he said he loved so much were born, and he didn't know a single one of their birthdays.

I went back into the courtroom for the sentencing, which was even more awful than I'd imagined it would be. I didn't realise they'd read out the details of what he'd done, so I was shocked when the judge said, 'Count one,' then actually described what he'd been found guilty of – I don't think any of us expected that.

I kept glancing at Tom and he looked terrible. In fact, I've never seen anybody look the way he did – I thought he was going to be sick. Then suddenly I thought, 'Now, more than at any other time, I *have* to be strong.' So I did what I always do in emotional situations, and didn't show any emotion at all. It didn't mean I didn't feel anything, it was just that I was determined not to let *him* see that I was upset.

I'm embarrassed to say that I was also upset when I heard he was dying – I think we all were. What I couldn't work out was *why* I felt the way I did, when all I'd wanted to do since the day Heidi told me what had happened was hang him from the nearest yardarm. I was disgusted with myself.

When I bumped into Lesley in town one day, I asked her what she thought might be the reason for my inappropriate reaction to the news. Of course, as Heidi's counsellor, Lesley couldn't counsel me, but she did explain that the brain is like a sponge and that it holds all the good things as well as the bad. 'You can't control what comes forward,' she told me. 'And when you heard he was dying, you remembered the good things.' I suppose she was right, because the life we'd had before he changed was lovely.

For a while, I even toyed with the idea of going to see him in the hospice. I know Heidi did too, and that she was sorry afterwards because she didn't go. So maybe it was the same for her, in that it wasn't only the bad things that came forward. I don't think either of us realised he'd die so soon though, and we expected to have more time to decide. But I'm sure we'd have been disappointed if we had gone to see him, because I don't think he'd ever have said he was sorry, which is what you're really hoping for in a situation like that, so that you can have some kind of closure.

Who can explain any of it? I've gone over it in my head a million times and I simply can't understand it. They were *his* children. Is it some sort of control thing for men like him, rather than something purely sexual? I think he felt like he was controlling me, too, when he did something to Heidi upstairs, for example, and then came down and put his arms around me.

When we were married he often used to talk about his childhood, about how strict his dad was, and how he used to hit him with his belt. I never knew whether or not that was true, but even if it was, it's no excuse for what he did.

He was the sort of person who always had to be 'top dog'. He'd joke around with the lads who used to help him carry his equipment to gigs and shows, but even when they were mucking about, he had to be number one. It was the same thing with the children: he'd play-fight with them when they were young, but *he* always had to be the winner.

Sometimes, he'd tie the children up when he was rough and tumbling with them. He'd use his dressing-gown cord to tie their ankles behind their backs, so that their feet were almost touching their bottoms. Then he'd tie their hands together with the same chord and say, 'Now, get out of that.' Dan, the policeman who was such a support to us later, told me it's called hog-tying and that it's a sexual thing some men do.

I'd never seen or heard of it before – I just knew I hated him doing it to the children. But whenever I said anything about it, he'd be impatient with me and ask what I was getting so fussed up about, so I thought *I* was the idiot. Apart from not liking it, however, it didn't seem significant in any way at the time.

Something that really shocked me later was knowing that he had said to Heidi, 'You mustn't tell Mum. It's our little secret.' I've seen things on TV in recent years and apparently that's something they often say. But it was just horrible to know he'd actually used those words with Heidi.

I tell myself I should have been more aware. But I didn't even know at that time that there was anything to be aware *of*, because I didn't know there were men who did that sort of thing to anyone's children, let alone to their own. The police used to come to the house when they were compiling a case against him and say things like, 'We're so busy, we're working flat out.' And I used to wonder, 'Busy doing *what*?' Even when we went to court and there was a mother and her children waiting to use the little private room after us, I was shocked to think that another man was on trial for doing the same sort of thing he had done.

I've met other people since then who have talked to me about their experiences because they know it happened to us, so I do realise now just how common it is. But I had no idea at the time.

We were lucky with the support we had. Dan, the policeman, was a lovely man, and so easy to talk to. And Lesley was wonderful too – she was always really good about picking us up and taking us to the police station. I know she has been incredibly supportive of Heidi as well.

Chloe didn't like Heidi's counsellor, although I think that was more to do with her not liking the fact that Lesley knew, rather than anything to do with Lesley herself. Then, unfortunately, when the people at social services said Chloe had to have some sort of counselling, she didn't have the good experience Heidi has always had with Lesley.

Because Chloe was just 11, she was too young to have adult counselling, and too old for the child counselling she did have, which involved them saying things to her like, 'This is a sad face. This is a happy face. Do you know the difference?' It was completely wrong for Chloe and I think it put her off counselling altogether. But there didn't seem to be anything available that was in between the two.

Whenever I think about what happened to Heidi and Chloe, I still ask myself 'Why?' We had a nice marriage and everything was normal – as far as I was aware, anyway. So why this? I don't think there is any answer though, or certainly not one we'll ever know.

Luckily, I can discuss things with my children quite openly. I've talked about it, in different ways, with all of them, although more with Heidi than with Tom or Chloe. I've said many times to Heidi and to Chloe that I wish they'd felt they could tell me. But, as Heidi explained to me, 'It was because I was so close to you, Mum. I didn't want to hurt you. He said he'd have to leave if I told you, and I didn't want that to happen. I didn't want the family to be split up.'

I've told Tom that I really feel as though I let him down, because although Heidi and I had planned to tell him what had happened before the police arrested his dad, we didn't get to him in time. I think he understands that now, and realises that I couldn't say anything because he was living with him.

I had a fairly normal childhood – Dad went to work, Mum did the cooking and the housework, and nothing particularly exciting ever happened. That was the sort of childhood I wanted for my children, and I feel awful that I didn't give it to them.

In fact, my three children are all quite different.

I think Heidi needed the closure of this book. She's been writing bits on and off for a long time, and I really hope it will help her now that it's done.

Chloe always said she only went to the funeral to check that he was in the box! But she's good at hiding her feelings, so I'm not sure that's true.

For Tom, his dad was his hero, as dads are for most little boys. It must have been hard for him to have to face the fact that he wasn't the man Tom had always thought he was.

For me, this was somebody I put my trust in, 100 per cent. What an idiot I was! That's what I feel now, anyway.

But you can't live your life not trusting anybody – you'd be a nervous wreck if you did that, and nobody would ever get married. It hasn't made it difficult for me to trust other people, though. For example, my new partner Ted plays with my grandchildren, although I suppose I might feel less confident about that if it wasn't for the fact that he's got children of his own who love him and who visit him because they want to.

I've forgotten a lot of what happened during that time – I think it was all so shocking that my mind has blocked it out. Perhaps it's a defence mechanism. In fact, I think if Heidi hadn't been so intent on writing this book, I wouldn't think about any of it at all. At least, I *hope* I wouldn't. Although I haven't let my children see it – except very occasionally when I've got a bit tearful in front of Heidi – it caused me countless hours of anguish. But in the end you have to say to yourself, 'It's a horrible part of my life, but it's time to move on.'

I think Heidi would like me to show my feelings more. But I can't. I used to think, 'If I let go now, I'll go to pieces.' And I knew I couldn't allow myself to do that, to be the one breaking down and weeping, when there were things that had to be done. You just have to keep going.

When we were seeing the counsellor and talking to the police it felt as though it was all happening to someone else, as though I was reading about it in a magazine, for example. I think I must have been particularly naive, not knowing that sort of thing happened to normal people – people like us.

It makes my blood run cold when I think about how I used to let the RAC man take Tom into the toilet when we were shopping in town. Tom had got to an age when he wanted to go into the men's toilet on his own, and one day this man, who was always in his little stall outside the supermarket, said, 'I'll take your son in, if you want.' You wouldn't let someone do that these days – and they wouldn't offer. I did ask Tom when I remembered about the RAC man after all this happened, and he assured me that it was fine. But I can't believe now that I did that, when I didn't know the man at all.

As things turned out, the man I *should* have been wary of wasn't a stranger, but my own husband, who was a man I thought I knew very well.

What We Know Now

Although it would be nice to believe that at least some people who have been abused as children can just shrug it off and get on with their adult lives as if nothing had ever happened, that's probably rarely, if ever, the case. What happened to us will affect many aspects of our lives forever. But although it's true that we all find it very difficult to trust people and are constantly alert to any possibility that our children are coming into contact with 'unvetted' adults, there are some more positive effects too. For example, as well as being determined to ensure that our own children's lives are happy and secure, they know already that they can talk to us at any time about *anything*.

Writing this book has involved some *eureka* moments for all of us. For example, realising that some of the assumptions we had made about each other's feelings and reactions were actually based on misconceptions and misunderstandings, and that you can't ever really know what someone else is thinking, feeling or experiencing unless you ask them, and then listen to what they tell you. Another revelation was that we are more similar to each other than we thought.

Another, that despite our initial trepidation, there's a calmness that comes with knowing, which is almost like finding your centre of gravity at last.

What we have also learned is to accept the fact that none of the things that happened when we were children were the fault of any of us, and that hiding things and not speaking out is never the best thing to do, even if you believe, rightly or wrongly, that your silence is protecting someone you love. When you're a child or a teenager and something bad is happening to you, you might think that the people you care about will suffer if you reveal a secret you've been told to keep. But the reality is that no one who loves you would want you to suffer either. And no child should be asked to keep a secret.

Heidi, Tom and Chloe

Chloe

I have just read the whole book for the first time, from start to finish, in one sitting. It's amazing! I can't believe how much better it's made me feel in my head. I don't know if that's because everything is so much clearer now that I've read about what happened to Heidi and Tom. Or if it's due to the fact that Heidi's side of things makes so much more sense to me now. We have so many similarities, even today, in our normal lives, which I didn't have any idea were related to what happened to us when we were younger. I hope Heidi and Tom are as happy with our book as I am.

When Heidi asked me to tell my story, I really didn't want to do it. I only agreed because when I thought about it I realised I owed her an explanation. The truth is, though, I was dreading it. But, by the end of the process, I had completely changed my mind. This is the email I've just sent her.

I've just finished reading the book! It made me laugh, cry and mostly appreciate how loved I was by you. Thank you for being you, Heidi, because without you, there most definitely wouldn't have been me, or my family, or our strong family unit as it stands today. You broke the silence, which was shit for a long time, but you helped us all by telling the truth.

It makes me think of that film *The Butterfly Effect*. Where would we all be now if you hadn't found my diary? I certainly believe that I would have killed myself, as I didn't know that anything he was doing was wrong. And if I had realised it was when I was young, I probably would have ended it, or turned to drink or drugs to block out the memories. So, in hindsight, I realise that you saved me and that you actually are the superhero you always thought you were!

Thank you for being my sister, and thank you for being you, because without you there, I and my children would not exist and I wouldn't have the fantastic life I have now. ♡

Tom

The process of writing and reading this book has highlighted for me that things of this nature can very easily be left in the past without there being any consequences for the offenders. Impacted people don't want to talk about what happened to them, either because they're scared or because it makes them feel uncomfortable, which is understandable. But as bad as it feels to talk about it, remember that the true scariest moments have passed, and that when you stand up and shout out, people *will* listen and it *will* stop.

Knowing what I know now, I wish I could go back in time and be the one to shout out for my sisters, but I can't. So I just want to say that if this book strikes a chord with someone out there who has a suspicion or knows something, don't sit back and hope it will all work out. Call someone, speak to someone, email, tweet, Facebook. Get it out there! Someone will hear you.

The only way to be aware of the signs of things happening in a house that should be full of trust is not to be scared of recognising those things. We all have a duty to look around and be objective, as difficult and as painful as that might be, because these things *do* happen and they're not going to stop happening unless we do something.

That being said, today's world is very different from the world my sisters and I grew up in. There's more awareness and understanding of these issues now, although still nowhere near enough. We all have skeletons in our closets, and that's okay. It's when those skeletons affect other people that you, me, everyone, needs to stand up and shout.

My sisters went through a huge ordeal when they were younger, an ordeal that bled into later years and still affects the decisions and choices they make today. I have great admiration for them both. They are a testament to our family and they show strength that cannot be measured, only understood and respected.

Heidi

When I was in my teens, I used to search the library for anything that might enable me to make some sort of sense of my experiences, or at least to feel as though I wasn't the only person in the world all those things had happened to, but I didn't really know what I was looking for. Now, I realise that it was this book – or something very like it. So I hope that when another girl is searching another library, she will find the book we've written and know that she is not alone.

There was so much I didn't know about Chloe's and Tom's experiences that it was surreal, as well as heartbreaking, to read their chapters, and what Mum had written. What amazing people they are, to have agreed to tell their stories because they wanted to help me have closure. I felt selfish for asking them to do it, and I feel incredibly privileged to have them in my life. I hope they know now, from reading my story, that they were always at the forefront of my mind in everything I did. I have great love, admiration and respect for them, and I am proud of them for the way they fought their battles.

I've learned that Tom and Chloe are much stronger than I thought they were. So maybe I *should* back off and let them manage their own affairs, rather than trying to take charge when they're perfectly happy and able to cope on their own, with the help and support of their own partners and children.

Something else I understand now – which might seem obvious to other people – is that just because someone doesn't talk about their emotions, it doesn't mean they don't have any, or that they haven't been deeply affected by things that have happened to them in the past. Knowing that my mother and siblings care about me means more to me than anyone will ever understand. Although it might seem as though I have created strength out of what happened to me – to all of us – the truth is that I struggle every day not to give in to the anxiety I feel, or to the heartbreak, pain and sadness that sometimes threaten to overwhelm me and that can occasionally result in bouts of severe depression. I am lucky, too, to have the love and support of my husband and daughter.

Out of the wreckage of our childhood, Tom, Chloe and I have built lives that revolve around our own amazing immediate and extended families of nephews and nieces. I am proud to say that, despite everything, we will never allow ourselves to be beaten by the past and the future is bright for us all.

Thank you, Chloe and Tom, for being people I am proud to call my sister and brother, and for helping me to make my dream of writing our story a reality.

A Footnote to Our Story

Heidi

It took me a while to decide whether or not to add this footnote to our story, particularly in view of the fact that we want to encourage people to speak out about child abuse. In the end, though, I decided that it would be dishonest not to disclose it. And, fortunately, Dan – the policeman who we first met at the 'safe house' we went to when Chloe was 11, where she locked herself in the toilet and refused to give a statement – is by no means a true representative of the many good policemen and other people whose job it is to offer help and support to victims of child abuse.

Dan continued to be a huge support for us all for quite some time after that first meeting. He really seemed to care about us and I ended up trusting him completely, which isn't something that comes easily to anyone who has been abused as a child by their own father. Then, one day, not very long ago, Lesley phoned me to break the news that Dan had been arrested on charges related to child pornography.

I was so shocked, I don't think I could really take in what she was saying. But when it finally did sink in, I was incredibly upset.

When Dan's case went to trial, he was given a suspended sentence and was quoted in the newspapers as saying how ashamed he felt for having let his family down. I don't suppose he'll ever read this book, and he probably wouldn't recognise himself if he did, as we haven't used the real names of anyone mentioned in it, to preserve their anonymity. But if he does ever read it, I'd like him to know how devastated I was when I heard what he'd been doing. I can understand why he feels badly for his family. What I hope *he* understands is that he also let down every vulnerable, sexually abused child who ever placed their fragile trust in him.

Acknowledgements

We would like to express our gratitude to our publisher, Random House, and to all the other people who have helped make this book a reality. We would also like to thank Lesley and the counsellors at Childline, our families for their love and encouragement, and our mum for being supportive of the book and of each of us individually as we told our stories, even though, sometimes, it can't have been easy for her.

Heartfelt thanks also go to Jane, who worked hard to bring together our stories in such a personal way.

Last but not least, thank you to all the people working for social services, the police and the courts to help support children and adults who have suffered abuse, and to the survivors of abuse who find the courage to speak out.

Childline

Phone calls are free to: 0800 1111

Website: www.childline.org.uk

About the Authors

Chloe is a full-time mum to her three children. She is 29 and lives on the south coast with her partner.

Tom is 34, has two children and works as a business team leader. He is a passionate fisherman who says he could never live far from the sea.

Heidi is 36 and lives with her husband and daughter in London, where she works as an events manager and as a voluntary ambassador for a children's charity.

Jane Smith is a ghostwriter and author of more than 30 published books, many of which have been *Sunday Times* top ten bestsellers. www.janesmithghostwriter.com